The Woman
Behind the Collar

Is not this the fast that I choose:
    to loose the bonds of injustice,
    to undo the thongs of the yoke,
to let the oppressed go free,
    and to break every yoke?
Is it not to share your bread with the hungry,
    and bring the homeless poor into your house;
when you see the naked, to cover them,
    and not to hide yourself from your own kin?
Then your light shall break forth like the dawn,
    and your healing shall spring up quickly;
your vindicator shall go before you,
    the glory of the LORD *shall be your rear guard.*
Then you shall call, and the LORD *will answer;*
    you shall cry for help, and he will say, Here I am.
If you remove the yoke from among you,
    the pointing of the finger, the speaking of evil,
if you offer your food to the hungry
    and satisfy the needs of the afflicted,
then your light shall rise in the darkness
    and your gloom be like the noonday.
The LORD *will guide you continually,*
    and satisfy your needs in parched places,
    and make your bones strong;
and you shall be like a watered garden,
    like a spring of water,
    whose waters never fail.
Your ancient ruins shall be rebuilt;
    you shall raise up the foundations of many generations;
you shall be called the repairer of the breach,
    the restorer of streets to live in.

—Isaiah 58:6–12

The Woman
Behind the Collar

The Pioneering Journey
of an Episcopal Priest

JOY CARROLL WALLIS

A Crossroad Book
The Crossroad Publishing Company
New York

The author and publisher are grateful to the following for permission to use their copyright material:

Page 136, Outside Church House with the bishop of Dover © Paul Grover/ Telegraph Group; pages 149, 155, and 178, photographs © BBC Picture Archives; page 168, newspaper article © *The Daily Mirror*; page 216, Joy Carroll Wallis on her wedding day with Dawn French © Atlantic Syndication Partners; pages 260, 261, and 265, photographs © Gerald Martineau.

All other photographs are from the author's personal collection. While every effort has been made to trace the owners of copyright material produced herein, the publishers apologize for any omissions and are prepared to incorporate missing acknowledgments in any future editions.

Cover photo © Roy Robinson

The Crossroad Publishing Company
481 Eighth Avenue, New York, NY 10001

First published by HarperCollins*Entertainment* 2002
Copyright © Joy Carroll Wallis 2002

Crossroad edition published 2004

Printed in the United States of America

The text is set in 11/14 Sabon. Display type is Isadora.

Library of Congress Cataloging-in-Publication Data
Wallis, Joy Carroll.
    The woman behind the collar : the pioneering journey of an Episcopal priest / Joy Carroll Wallis.
        p. cm.
    ISBN 0-8245-2265-6 (alk. paper)
    1. Wallis, Joy Carroll. 2. Episcopal Church – Clergy – Biography.
3. Clergy – United States – Biography. 4. Ordination of women. I. Title.
BX5995.W342A3 2004
283′.092 – dc22
                                                                    2003025370

1 2 3 4 5 6 7 8 9 10   10 09 08 07 06 05 04

For Luke and Jack

Contents

A Word from TV's Vicar of Dibley, Dawn French

Joy Carroll. What a name. Charles Dickens (who loved to invent names for his characters which perfectly encapsulated their personalities or their jobs) couldn't have concocted a more apt nomenclature. "Joy" is right for someone whose heart is so full of optimism and hope, and "Carroll" conjures up images of Christmas and songs and church. Hooray — the right girl was fitted with the right name. Well done, parents.

I almost didn't believe that was her real name when Richard Curtis first told me about Joy. I thought he was simply suggesting a possible name for the character he had asked me to play in his latest sitcom, *The Vicar of Dibley*. Even then, I thought the name was a bit too perfect, too suitable for a female vicar.

He then explained that Joy was a living, breathing girl vicar and, what's more, she was willing to meet us and answer any questions. It was a great opportunity, especially since I had been having seriously cold feet about the series, precisely because I couldn't imagine a female priest who was young enough, or spunky enough, or credible enough, to base the character on. Very often this doesn't matter with a sitcom; in fact it's usually better to totally invent the character, especially if she is supposed to be hyper-real anyway, with the kind of personality extremes that are irresistibly funny — you know, the monstrous Edina Monsoon, the selfish Patsy, the pompous Basil Fawlty, the arrogant Frasier Crane, the cowardly Larry Sanders, etc. The difference with the *Vicar* scripts was that Geraldine, while not totally flawless, was essentially a good, honest, intelligent central force, while the more overtly comic characters floated around and in and out of the stories. I felt that, unless I could somehow "ground" the character in reality, the rest wouldn't work. (I remember mooting the idea of playing Alice Tinker instead at one point, since I could see the route to those jokes more clearly!) To try and make Gerry more natural, I knew it would help to meet someone like her, someone whose experience I could plunder.

There were, of course, two added incentives:

1. I could sharpen my prying skills by asking lots of personal questions. (Are vicars allowed to sleep with their boyfriends? Do they take the pill? Are buckteeth and stutters compulsory?)

2. Fantastic excuse to eat cake.

So I went to meet Joy.

First, you should know that she's a babe. I didn't expect that. I don't know why I didn't expect that, but I didn't. I immediately liked her, and felt totally relaxed in her company. She laughed a lot, and I knew that it would be okay to ask her anything, and I did. I was struck by her warm benevolence. She was interested and interesting, without being at all patronizing. She seemed to me to be a very modern humanitarian, with a proper understanding of politics and pop in equal measures. Her home was simple and friendly, and there were sufficient empties lined up in the kitchen to reassure me that this girl knew how to party. In fact, she was the sort of person I would choose to be my friend. One other characteristic really impressed me: she rooted everything she thought and did in her faith. It seemed to me that her belief was, and is, the unshakeable rock on which she has built her life, and I couldn't help but be in awe of her certainty.

A few weeks later, I went with Joy to see her conduct a funeral. The elderly chap who had lost his wife was obviously distraught, and I watched as Joy climbed down from the pulpit, took his hand in hers, and spoke quietly with him for some time. In that moment, as I witnessed her tender compassion and saw the genuine comfort she gave that man, I knew something was undeniably true. I knew that it was so right that women should be ordained. Women are good at this job, it comes naturally to us, providing spiritual guidance and succor. We do it all the time in our everyday lives and, what's more, we like doing it. Yep, I could finally see how Dibley's "Geraldine" might just work after all.

Joy was the consultant for the show, and she gave us lots of advice about all sorts of things, spiritual and practical. How should we dress the altar for a service at Easter? When is it appropriate to wear the dog collar? How do you wear a dog collar with a dress? What would be a suitable reading during a service for animals? Is eating five giant Toblerones in a row a sin? Do sinners actually burn in hell? Or will a strict telling off suffice? And on and on.... But, more than this, Joy was the inspiration, and she continues to be just that for so many people, as this book reveals. I notice that Joy writes as she speaks: very honest, human, and anecdotal. Incidentally, she preaches in this way too. Her driving force is her desire to connect with people, to make lasting bonds and to make a difference. She's certainly made a difference to my life. Long may she continue to inspire everyone she meets. Go, girlfriend.

Dawn French

A Word from the Archbishop of Canterbury, Dr. Rowan Williams

One of the things that clergy have to get used to is the fact that they carry around with them a cloud of fantasies and images from other people's minds. It isn't always easy to keep the truth about yourself in view when you're surrounded by the legacy of generations of stories and portraits of what it is to be a cleric. And every generation produces a few fresh refinements of the fantasy.

What I found most enriching and challenging in Joy's book was the way in which she puts the question of how we might engage positively, not negatively, with this fact. Can we ourselves as Christians and as Christian ministers both recognize this powerful and emotionally charged process of projection around us and do something with it that will help communicate what we hope to communicate? Joy took this brave step of assisting in the formation of some new images — and the results are familiar. It is extraordinary to see just how rapidly respect and affection toward women clergy have grown in popular culture, simply through the presentation of a warm, fallible, and faithful priest in a sitcom!

Like so many of her generation of women clergy in Britain and the United States, she has had to shape a new perception about "vicars." And like them too, she knows what the cost is of living so long within a church where images of women have been so often a source of frustration or an assault on proper self-esteem. This is not only a book about how one woman cleric helped to shift perceptions of the clergy in society at large; it is also, less obviously but very deeply, about the perceptions and images that free us or keep us prisoner in a much wider context — about how the church when it is doing its job is in the business of restoring, deepening, and strengthening what it is that people are allowed to say and sense about themselves. It is about how the gospel shows us that we can let ourselves be redescribed and redefined, once we know that God sees us whole and sees us with love and promise.

The final words of this book are "the image of God in humanity." This is appropriate. Ultimately, we are not called to refine our image to the point where we and our society are satisfied with it — though that's the message we constantly pick up in the media these days. We are called to let ourselves be refined by the relentless action of grace and mercy until we reflect back to God something of the divine nature. This story of a journey toward ordination and beyond is not a cozy narrative of how the world learned to love women clergy, but a serious challenge to look at how we come to terms with the images people have of us and move freely within those perceptions and expectations, using them creatively, and yet not trapped by them. It is a story in which the importance of women's vocations is part of a bigger picture about the freedom the gospel brings.

A serious challenge, yes — but seriously entertaining as well. A very human record, and all the more transparent to the divine for being so. Which is not something Christians should find so surprising, given the central story they tell of how God has been present with us.

Rowan Williams

Prologue

"I ask that you greet the results, whatever they might be, with a dignified silence." Tension filled the debating chamber of Church House in Westminster. George Carey, the archbishop of Canterbury, was about to put an end to the agonizing wait. I had not moved all day from my seat. My body cried out for food, coffee, and painkillers for my pounding headache, but I wanted to hear every word spoken for and against the motion to ordain women to the priesthood of the Church of England.

At the end of the debate, we voted. I rose to my feet and moved toward a large oak door engraved with the words "Clergy Ayes." On either side of the door stood tellers carefully counting each body that passed through. My hands were sweating, and my heart was beating wildly. This was the precious vote I had been elected to cast. Just as I reached the door I had a fleeting moment of panic and checked that I was going through the right door. This was not the time to make that kind of mistake!

The three houses — Bishops, Clergy, and Laity — each had to secure a two-thirds majority for the motion to pass, and we knew it would be close. On the other side of the doors, in the circular corridor surrounding the chamber, those who had voted spoke in hushed tones to one another. I stood beside one of my women colleagues, a good friend from the Manchester diocese. She whispered to me with a look of agony on her face, "It feels like we've been pregnant all this time, preparing for new birth, and now, at the last minute, we're not sure whether the baby will be born alive or dead."

As I moved around the corridor, I passed those who had come through the "Clergy Noes" door. It was then that I saw Father Andrew Burnham, my great friend on Synod who was against the ordination of women. We had vowed to respect each other's position and to remain friends throughout. We looked at each other in this clear moment of difference, having come through different doors, and we hugged. Though we didn't yet know the outcome of our votes, we were both aware of the pain that one of us would soon feel.

After what felt like hours, we were all summoned back into the chamber. Into the silence, the archbishop now read the numbers that had been handed to him.

> House of Bishops 39 for, 13 against.
> House of Clergy 176 for, 74 against.
> House of Laity 169 for, 82 against.

We madly tried to do the math. Had it passed or not? We weren't sure. The numbers were so close in the House of Laity. My stomach clutched as the archbishop spoke the words, "The motion is passed."

We had in fact just achieved the two-thirds majority in the House of Laity by *one* vote! If one layperson had voted the other way, the whole process would have to be set aside until a new synod was elected. There would have been no women priests in England for another five to ten years. It was amazingly close and took a few seconds to sink in. In the "dignified silence," I and other women clergy around me beamed and threw our hands in the air with tears of joy and relief streaming down our faces. It was finally settled. We could now get back to the work of ministry without being sidetracked. As one of my colleagues, Bernice Broggio, once put it, we had been "common-law priests" and now, on November 11, 1992, the church had decided to "make honest women of us."

The Movement for the Ordination of Women had hired the Methodist Central Hall. Many women deacons, congregation members, and their families were gathered there, as were my parents. They had listened to and watched the debate as the proceedings were relayed via big video screens. The result took them by surprise. A wave of emotion swept through the crowd as small groups hugged one another and tears flowed with unreserved joy.

Outside Church House another crowd had gathered. They had been listening on the radio and watching on portable TVs. As the results were announced, the silent waiting crowd erupted with screams and cheers. Champagne corks flew across the yard and songs of joy were sung. People danced and hugged. The party continued on into the night. As I sat in the chamber, in the dignified silence, I knew exactly where I would rather have been.

At the age of twenty-nine, I was the youngest member of the House of Clergy in the General Synod. I had been elected by my colleagues in the diocese of Southwark to serve for five years, from 1990 to 1995. It was in those five years that the historic decision was made to ordain women to the priesthood of the Church of England. I went on to become one of the first women to be ordained into the priesthood in England. I was privileged to help prepare for it, to witness it first hand, and to pioneer those first years as the church received women as priests.

I was blissfully unaware that, before long, I would become known as "the real vicar of Dibley" when the hit TV show, written by Richard Curtis and starring Britain's premier comedienne Dawn French, burst onto our screens.

Chapter One

The Vicar's Daughter

When I was born, my mother prayed, "Lord, help me to remember that she is yours and simply on loan to me." A few weeks later, Mum pushed the big pram proudly down the street, smiling as passersby cooed at the newborn baby girl. She parked me outside the small row of shops (which was apparently quite safe in those days) and proceeded to do her shopping. About an hour later she arrived home. She rang the doorbell. My dad opened the door to see my mum laden down with shopping. "Where's Joy?" he asked with concern. "Joy?" Mum's eyes grew wide with panic. "Joy! I left her outside the shops!" She ran back at the speed of lightning and found me where she had left me, still being cooed at by all who passed by. Perhaps her prayer should have been, "Lord, help me to remember that she is yours *and* mine."

My parents, John and Thelma Carroll, were pioneers. They pulled down old churches and built new ones, both literally and metaphorically. I was born in the Princess Christian Nursing Home in Slough, but, by the time I was eighteen months old, we had moved to South Lambeth, where my dad was to be the vicar of St. Stephen's Church. You might say I imbibed the inner city from the cradle.

Me, at eighteen months old, in the old vicarage garden, South Lambeth.

On the day of our arrival at Number 16, St. Stephen's Terrace, I made my first lasting friend. The vicarage at St. Stephen's was old. My mother tried to open a long-closed window that refused to budge. As she pushed with the palm of her hand, her hand slipped from the frame and went straight through the glass. Blood spurted from Mum's wrist. The vicarage phone had not yet been connected. Dad had to think quickly.

Earlier in the day, he had noticed an elderly lady in the yard next door. Quickly, he handed me over the fence to this woman — a complete stranger — and raced down the street to a phone booth to call an ambulance. The ambulance rushed my mum to St. Thomas's Hospital, where they stitched her up. In the meantime, I was getting to know the old woman whom I later called "Auntie Hudson." Over the next few years I was a regular visitor to her basement flat, where she indulged me with sweets and chocolate, read me nursery rhymes, and, when I was a little older, comics. I was heartbroken when Auntie Hudson became too old to look after herself and moved to Scotland to live with her son.

South Lambeth was the home of an elderly generation, many of whom were theater entertainers. Auntie Hudson's husband had been a well-known singer in the music halls; she had met him when she was a chorus girl. Most of these artists were facing hard times as the local music halls closed due to the arrival of television. One of the nearest to us was the New Cross Empire, and, despite its glorious past — George Formby had often topped the bill there — it was closed in 1954 and demolished in 1958.

As well as being home to people like Auntie Hudson, South Lambeth was an increasingly multicultural but economically deprived inner-city neighborhood. The white working class lived alongside a large community of first-generation immigrants from the West Indies. Housing consisted mainly of small flats carved out of large, once fashionable Victorian houses on Albert Square and the surrounding streets. This comparatively small enclave was in turn surrounded by large, poor-quality housing estates. Most of the blocks of flats on these estates were built to be five stories high in order to escape the regulation that buildings six stories or higher required the inclusion of lifts. There was the occasional exception when a tower block would rise to twenty or more stories. Play areas for children were almost nonexistent, and the little space available was usually occupied by frustrated young skinheads wearing their uniform of "bovver boots" and braces.*

---

*Slang term for black heavy foots (used for kicking others) and suspenders.

It soon became apparent that we had a lot to learn
about the community we had moved into. At the age of
two, my lullaby was the blaring music from the pub across
the road. One Saturday night, as I had just fallen asleep,
my father was putting the final touches on his sermon for
the next day. He could hear the usual angry shouts as
drunken young men brawled outside. All of a sudden, he
heard something different. There was now screaming outside on the street and someone was banging on the front
door. My dad opened the door, where a neighborhood
man was holding a tuft of hair saying, "My wife has just
pulled this from my mistress's head, what shall I do?"

On another Sunday evening, while on their way to
church, my parents saw a man beating up a woman in the
street. She screamed in agony and fear. My brave father
ran to the scene. He bent down to the ground beside the
woman and told the man to kick him but leave the woman
alone. My dad then called to my mother, "Thelma, call
the police." Suddenly, to his surprise, the woman turned
on him and yelled, "Why don't you piss off and mind
your own business?" She then got up and walked away
with her husband, arm in arm.

To think of oneself as a messiah who had come to
save people clearly would not work. Fortunately, it wasn't
my parents' style to live like missionaries in a deprived
neighborhood. They knew their ministry would have to
be a two-way street of receiving as well as giving. They
threw themselves in at the deep end, making local friends.
While many clergy sent their children to private schools,
my younger brother and I were sent to the local state
school.

The vicarage was a big old house and a nightmare to
heat and clean. It sat next to the enormous Victorian

church that was built to seat thousands but had a congregation of only eleven. In order to build a congregation
and get to know the people in the parish, my dad, still
young and energetic, went into the housing estates where
boys kicked around footballs in the courtyards. He joined
in their games and soon organized them into teams. Before long, we had a youth club on our hands and some of
the children's parents began to turn up at church to find
out more about this new young vicar. As the church grew,
so did I.

My brother, Ray, was born when I was three years old
and became the first victim of my bossy nature. When I
saw him having his diaper changed, I made an immediate
decision that it was time to stop wearing diapers at night
as "diapers were for babies." I was a big girl now and believed myself to be "in charge" of Ray. I enjoyed having
someone around to organize, but sometimes I pushed the
limits. When he had finally suffered enough of my dom-
inance, my sweet-natured sibling would have to rise up
and fight me to survive. I also had a habit of "organizing" the other kids in the street and one day, when my
mum saw me standing in the middle of a group of boys,
showing them how to pump up a football, she ran for the
camera to record the moment.

Our large vicarage yard was the envy of the neighborhood kids, who had nothing more than a balcony to call
their own. It was constantly filled with children from
the flats who used it like it was a playground. I quickly
learned to share, but wasn't always very gracious about
it. "I'm going to the bathroom I'd call. "I'm putting my
bat in this spot and if any of you dare touch it, I'll smash
your face in." I ran indoors to pee, only to be met by my
irate father, who had heard what I said through an open

All in our Sunday best, my parents, John and Thelma Carroll, with my brother Ray and me.

window. He finished delivering his latest lecture on ethics to a six-year-old with the words, "and I never want to hear you speak to anyone like that again!"

At school I barely survived being "the vicar's daughter," but it toughened me up and certainly prepared me later in life for having my personal quirks manifested on TV in *The Vicar of Dibley*. Every week at school, my dad would come to lead an assembly. Every week I could have died from embarrassment. I was nudged and poked and ridiculed. It was just as bad as if I had a clown for a father. The rest of the week wasn't much better. If I was praised for doing something well, then I was called the "teacher's pet." If ever I was made a monitor or won a prize, it was "just because you're the vicar's daughter"! I hated it and put a lot of energy into trying to be as unlike a vicar's daughter as I could be. The naughtiest girl in the class was my best friend and, to prove that I could be naughty too, I once stuck my teacher's class keys together with very sticky bubble gum. I didn't care what my teachers thought of me but, like most ordinary kids, I wanted to be liked by my peers.

At home, too, I was an impish and strong-willed kid, which often got me into trouble. The old vicarage had no security system except for a series of hooks on each downstairs door, which my parents latched each night. If someone did manage to break into any of the rooms they would have to make noise and would struggle to get any further into the house. One day, Ray and I were playing in the hallway outside my dad's study. He had a visitor and one of us kids latched the hook outside his door, locking them in. The visitor turned out to be a con man who pulled out a knife. Dad struggled to get him out of the study, only to find that the door wouldn't open. Somehow he managed to get out, but he was furious with us. His anger, added to his fright, made him quite formidable. Once he had ejected the man, he came after us. "Which one of you put that hook over the door?" We both denied it. He asked the question again. We each said. "Not me." He got hold of us and proceeded to smack our legs in turn until one of us owned up. "Now I'm not smacking you for putting the hook over the door," he said. "I'm smacking you for lying."

I have no recollection of which one of us actually did it or which of us finally owned up, but I have never forgotten the incident. It was undoubtedly a sobering lesson for me that my antics had consequences and that it was never a good idea to lie or try to blame someone else when I'd made a mistake.

My parents, just like many other kids' parents, wanted to bring us up to be well-mannered and to know the difference between right and wrong. They taught us the importance of honesty, fairness, compassion, generosity, self-respect, and respect for others. In addition to these and other basic good values, I now believe that, as a vicar's kid in the inner city, I was learning other more unique lessons — lessons that equipped me for what God had planned for my life as an adult.

One of those lessons was the value of hospitality. As kids, Ray and I shared in my parents' ministry, especially when it came to having an open house. One day a young French couple knocked on our door. Speaking very little English, they asked if there was a hostel where they could stay. A few hours later, I moved in to share my brother's bedroom, and the French artist and his wife were ensconced in mine. They stayed for four weeks. As was always the case when we had guests, our cultural horizons were broadened and our understanding of the world around us was expanded. It was a privilege that I didn't always appreciate at the time.

Even though we were brought up in a working-class neighborhood with working-class friends, our exposure to so many interesting people and places allowed us to experience a childhood that is often available only to those from a middle-class background. With our feet firmly planted on the ground, our horizons were broad. We always had access to books and we had aware, informed, and articulate parents to encourage and guide us.

I always knew that life could have been very different if I had been born into a family without these benefits. The unfairness of that truth bothered me. Going to the local school and living in the same street as children who were poor certainly helped make me the person that I am today. I may have forfeited a pristine private school accent, but I learned the language of my peers. I hardly ever wore new clothes, but every year on my birthday I received a box in the mail from my godmother. Her daughter was exactly one year older than me and it was with sheer glee and excitement that I pored over the clothes I would be wearing in the coming year.

We never had any money for luxuries, but my parents were very creative and generous with what little they did have. One year I had the best birthday present ever — a second-hand, repainted, three-wheeler bike. I rode it proudly round and round the block every day for about three weeks. Then it was stolen from the garage. My parents couldn't afford to simply replace it, and it was a long time before I got another second-hand bike. I was upset for a while but I got over it. Looking back, it was in those early years that I began to understand that it wasn't always lots of new things that brought happiness. In biblical language, found in the book of Matthew, chapter 6, the lesson is:

> Do not store up for yourselves treasures on earth, where moth and rust destroy, and where thieves break in and steal. But store up for yourselves treasures in heaven... for where your treasure is, there your heart will be also.

Spending time together as a family was a priority for my parents. We children were never made to feel that we were second best to "God's work" or the church. I have some very happy memories of family fun. Every year on the night of the Eurovision Song Contest, we would all snuggle up in my parents' big bed and eat chocolate while we watched the songs performed on TV and the votes cast. The next day Dad would take us out to buy the record of the winning song. (The year that Cliff Richard won with "Congratulations" was the beginning of my life-long love of Cliff and his music!)

We often went to the seaside for our vacation and stayed with my dad's old aunt in Eastbourne. We'd get up at the crack of dawn to build boats in the sand before breakfast. I always noticed the retirement homes and the hotels along the seafront. It seemed strange to me that rows and rows of old people sat in rocking chairs behind the glass, knitting or simply gazing at the sea. "Dad, what are all those old people doing there?" I once asked. "Well," my dad tried to explain, "when people get very old, they like to spend time in beautiful places before they die." I went through many years of my childhood with a horrendous image of all those old people sitting there waiting to die. I was greatly disturbed by the thought that, as each one died, they would be removed from the chair and replaced with another person who would sit there until they died. As a child I obviously had a creative, if misguided imagination, but also a genuine concern for those old people. Little did I know then how intimately involved I would be with the pastoral care, life, and death of so many of my own elderly parishioners.

I also learned as a child that you can't always get what you want. For example, we were never allowed to have any pets. My dad always said that it was unfair to have a dog in the city. He also maintained, rather harshly, that pets were "a waste of time, money, and emotion." "Blessing of the animals" services and funerals for pets, which might be popular in parishes such as Dibley, were never a part of our inner-city church experience and, as kids, we could only dream about being a family that included animals.

One day a friend of my parents arrived with an unexpected gift for us kids: it was a cage with two gerbils in it. We were ecstatic. "Oh, Dad, can we keep them please?"

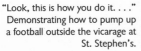

"Look, this is how you do it. . . ."
Demonstrating how to pump up
a football outside the vicarage at
St. Stephen's.

we begged. In order not to offend the friend, my father reluctantly agreed. We loved those gerbils. We fed them and filled their little water bottle. We spent hours watching them tear up toilet paper to make their bed, and we didn't care about the smell!

A few weeks later, Dad came to pick us up from school. On the way home, he said, "I have some good news and some bad news. Which do you want first?" "The good news!" we chorused. "Well," said Dad, "the good news is that the gerbils have had babies." "Hooray!" we yelled. "And the bad news is that the daddy gerbil has eaten them all." Our balloon immediately burst. Dad had disposed of the whole lot, and we were distraught. Our days of being pet lovers had been short lived, as Dad never gave in to our constant requests for a dog or a cat.

I never understood why Dad felt so strongly about having pets until I was in my thirties and heard what had happened to him as a child. When the Second World War broke out, Dad was not evacuated to the countryside like so many other children in London were. As an only child, he stayed at home in Blackheath throughout the Blitz. During that time, many families kept chickens — precious for their eggs and meat. My dad made special friends with one particular chicken that had a deformed wing. This little one was at the end of the pecking order and survived only because of his personal care. After a summer vacation in the country with an aunt, Dad returned home to find his friend served up on his plate for Sunday lunch. It was a shock that he never completely got over. I think he promised himself that he would never again get emotionally attached to an animal. I had mixed feelings when I first heard that story. I had to suppress a strong desire to laugh at the tragedy, but at the same time I felt sorry for my dad, who had been so wounded by his experience. Suddenly our "pet-less" upbringing made sense.

MY DAD NEVER did things by halves. When he believed that something was right, he made sure it happened. People either loved that or hated it. A monumental example of this was when, with Bishop Mervyn Stockwood's blessing, Dad and the Parochial Church Council decided to demolish the old St. Stephen's Church and build a new one.

Faced with an unmanageable building that was unable to impact the community, the Parochial Church Council enlisted a bright young architect to develop a plan. In place of the old church and vicarage would be built a more suitable vicarage and a smaller church, complete with a community center. There was so much land available that some of it was offered to St. Thomas's Hospital to use for rehousing purposes.

On the day of the steeple demolition, a crowd gathered to watch. It was a brave move to fly in the face of tradition and set the bulldozers to work tearing down the old Victorian church.

The vicarage, too, was razed to the ground and we moved to a temporary home while the new complex was being built. On Lambeth Palace Road, there is a tall house built over an archway at the entrance to Archbishop Temple School. This is where we lived for two years.

It was in that house, when I was nine years old, that we gathered around our black-and-white TV to watch Neil Armstrong be the first man to walk on the moon. All over the world, people witnessed that "giant leap," and their horizons were broadened. In my little corner of the planet, I watched as my dad helped St. Stephen's Church take its own giant leap. I began to learn the great lesson that the church is people, and people are always more important than buildings.

I had a fabulous view of the Houses of Parliament, Big Ben, and the archbishop of Canterbury's backyard from my bedroom window. For a couple of years, the noise from the pub across the road was gone, and it was the sound of Big Ben chiming that lulled me to sleep.

With Bishop Mervyn's regular encouragement, the new church, vicarage, and community center were completed and we moved back to our church neighborhood. At the end of November 1969, the bishop consecrated the whole complex to a fanfare of trumpets and joyous celebration.

A year later, the church was growing and the community center was the hub of the neighborhood. It housed a play group and youth groups and was well used by a variety of community groups. The church actively supported the South American Missionary Society, and every Sunday I sang in the choir, which wore turquoise, South American–style ponchos. As a young person, I experienced church to be colorful, exciting, welcoming, modern, and relevant. Why would anyone want anything less from a church? Life was good.

Every day, my parents read the Bible and prayed together at home. They believed that, through this, God would lead and guide them in their lives. One morning they read a passage from the book of Amos, chapter 6:

> Woe to them who take their ease in Zion . . . and care
> not for the plight of Joseph.

Things were going well at St. Stephen's and my parents were feeling comfortable. They pondered the Scripture they had just read and wondered if the time had come for a new challenge. The next morning the phone rang. It was the bishop: "John, what would you do if I offered you a dead church?"

Chapter Two

Growing and Changing

Big changes came in 1971. Britain went decimal, I started at St. Martin in the Fields High School for girls in Tulse Hill, and Dad was ready for a change of church. He always loved a challenge. The bishop of Southwark offered my father what he described as a "completely dead church." "If you take this on," said the bishop, "you will lift stones and find many worms — just replace them and say nothing!" The previous incumbent of St. Luke's, West Norwood, had not been a greatly loved man. He had remained in office many years past the normal retirement age (a situation that is no longer allowed in the Church of England), was rumored to have fiddled the books, and disliked children in church. Sadly, his body was found at the foot of Beachy Head Cliffs.

My twelve-year-old heart sank on our first Sunday at the new church. It looked like a dull and unfriendly place. There was a small choir with enthusiastic but dismal singers. The service was from the 1662 prayer book, which I endured but didn't understand. The congregation was mostly old people. It was, in fact, rather like a bigger, inner-city version of the Dibley parish church that Geraldine encountered when she arrived as the new priest in

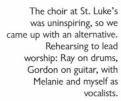

The choir at St. Luke's was uninspiring, so we came up with an alternative. Rehearsing to lead worship: Ray on drums, Gordon on guitar, with Melanie and myself as vocalists.

the first episode of *The Vicar of Dibley.* It didn't take me long, however, to spot some boys in the choir. "They look like they might be good for a laugh," I thought, and quickly joined. Soon I became friends with Gordon, Roger, Michael, and Diane; others were presently added to our number. None of us liked the choir much, but a solo of the Twenty-third Psalm could be sung at weddings and funerals for 50p. We began to plan and scheme ways to do something more exciting. Gordon, Diane, and I played the guitar and my brother, Ray, was learning to play the drums at school.

It was evident from an early age that Ray had rhythm. While I could sing and belonged to the school choir, he was the one who seemed to have music in his blood and bones. It started with the incessant drumming on the dining table with knives, forks, and spoons, which drove everyone crazy, and then progressed in his first year of secondary school to what seemed to be a more serious and focused commitment. He joined the percussion section of his school orchestra.

Rushing home from school one day, he handed Mum a leaflet advertising a concert. "Will you come?" Mum read the notice carefully. "Please..." he implored. And so it was that the three of us, Mum, Dad, and I, sat in the audience watching Ray in the orchestra. We waited to see him in action... and we waited. He was holding the cymbals and his greatest moment was at the end when, at the climax of "God Save the Queen," he got to crash them together just at the right moment!

The first single my brother ever bought was "Crocodile Rock" by Elton John. To encourage his interest in music and his enthusiasm for drumming, my parents bought him his drum kit. He turned out to be a natural and, from that time on, our house was always filled with the beat of his drums or sounds from *Top of the Pops*.

With Ray's set of drums, a couple of guitars and an enthusiastic group of teenagers, we were all set to form a music group. We also practiced some songs to sing in church. (Gordon was an avid Status Quo fan and I think he rather fancied that this might be the start of something big!)

"Pleeeeease, Dad, please let us have a spot on Sunday morning," I begged.

"Well," my dad said. "It has to be good. I'm trying to get rid of the choir. So it won't look good if we replace it with substandard music that isn't honoring to God."

"It will be good!" I promised.

We were ready... but was the church? As I remember, we certainly blew away some cobwebs as we led the congregation in worship that Sunday morning, and the offering of "modern music" was warmly received.

Our little group marked the beginning of a lot more changes that happened at St. Luke's. The church was gradually dragged into the twentieth century with the introduction of what we called Family Services. All the

services became less traditional and more relevant to ordinary people. New people would come and exclaim, "This
isn't what we expected church to be like — its great, we'll
come again!" And they did.

I have come to learn that change is never easy, especially when it happens in a church. Inevitably, there were
some members of St. Luke's who didn't like the new-style
services at all. I learned at an early age what all clergy discover at some point: some people just don't like change,
however positive, and will resist it with all their might.

My dad, together with a supportive core of church
members, was confident that a new, updated church was
what the community needed. They were determined not
to let a few traditionalists hold back progress. Sparks
inevitably flew, and some people left the church. Later,
at theological college, one of the things I learned was
that "tradition" is a good thing, but is often misunder-
stood. Tradition by its very nature changes with time. It's
rather like a river flowing from A to B. It twists, turns,
flows, and links us with the past. If our tradition never
moves or changes, it will become stagnant and unhealthy.
Change at St. Luke's was well overdue and was at times
painful. There was a cost, but the church was on the way
to revitalization and grew in numbers. Then we kids had
another idea.

"Let's start a youth club!" St. Luke's had a fabulous
crypt underneath the church. It was full of junk and in
a bad state of disrepair, but it had great potential. We
already met as a youth group on Sunday evenings at the
vicarage; it was a gathering for discussions, Bible study,
and social things. But this was to be something completely
different — a Saturday-night club that hopefully would
attract youth from all around.

We spent weeks cleaning up the crypt. The walls needed a few coats of paint; then we decorated them with our own graffiti. In one corner of the crypt, we set up a games area with pool and table tennis tables. A relaxing living-room area with old sofas and big, comfy chairs provided a cozy place to hang out and chat. There was a snack shop for refreshments, and best of all was the dance area. There was a big cage for the DJ and colored lighting flashed from the ceiling. The atmosphere was just right.

Some wonderful youth leaders emerged in the church, and so "Superlukes" was born. We were so proud of our great club. It was easy to invite friends from school to such a cool place, and soon it was a very popular venue.

Years later, after a good run, Superlukes had to be moved from the crypt because of fire and safety regulations. This was a tragedy as the crypt was 100 percent soundproof, which enabled us to play loud music without being a trouble to anyone else. The closure meant that large numbers of youth were now on the streets with nowhere to go, little to do, and so creating a seedbed for trouble. On hindsight, the local authority could have granted money to create a needed fire exit.

When I was sixteen, a group of us from St. Luke's Church formed a Christian band. Ray played his drums. There were two guitarists who played electric guitars, a flautist, and a line-up of five singers, of which I was one. We called ourselves "One Way."

The leader of the group wrote a lot of the songs we sang, and we rehearsed together every week. It became a serious commitment for all of us, and we performed concerts all over the country as well as at home in London. Once, we were even booked by a group of churches for an event in Wales, and, on occasions like this, we would

One Way gospel band, 1978.

load up the station wagons that two of the older members of the group owned.

Wedged in among all the equipment, we would joke, laugh, sing, and argue as we made our way to the next venue. They were great days and, for two years, we had a wonderful time playing and singing together. Perhaps in that time, we were sometimes able to communicate to our audiences about a God of justice, mercy, and love who might not be quite as unreachable as so many young people had been led to believe by the traditional church.

ST. MARTIN IN THE FIELDS High School for girls was the church school of the famous St. Martin in the Fields in Trafalgar Square, and we enjoyed a good relationship with the church and its vicar, the Reverend Austin Williams. Founders' Day services and Christmas Carol services were great events when the whole school boarded buses and filled the church to bursting. To this day, I cannot visit St. Martin's in Trafalgar Square without picturing the place full of schoolgirls in their chocolate-brown and red uniforms, complete with neat little hats.

At school, I belonged to a Christian group called Open House, which was run by our Religious Education teacher, Miss Sylvia Martin (who was also a deaconess in the Church of England). It was wonderfully open and a lot of fun. They organized regular Open House retreats, and we would go away for a few days to a country house conference center called Pilgrim Hall. This was a good time for me to explore my own understanding of God and Christianity, with a little independence from my parents. I especially enjoyed the discussions and question times when Reverend Williams joined us on the retreats. On returning from one such retreat, I surprised my parents as I excitedly described a powerful experience of the presence of God in a small local church. "We were sitting as a small group on the carpeted floor in front of the high altar. There was a candle in the middle to help us meditate in silence, and above us was a beautiful stained-glass window.

As I gazed at the candle, I felt transported by the silence as I sat with my friends. Suddenly the light changed and the sun came streaming through the brightly colored window, causing all kinds of beautiful beams to dance around us. I felt as though God was somehow meeting me in all these symbolic ways, in the light through the window, in the glow of the candle, in the presence of my friends, and in the silence."

I had never before experienced God in a mystical way, and it so impressed me, I couldn't wait to tell my parents. My evangelical upbringing meant that I was part of a tradition that downplayed the candles and the stained-glass windows, preferring words to silence; but they smiled and were pleased about my experience of God. I was grateful to Open House for introducing me as a young teenager to new ways of knowing God, although I actually still preferred modern worship and noise!

Years later, in 1994, eighty women from Southwark Diocese gathered on a retreat to prepare for ordination to the priesthood. Some women like me had been deacons for just a short time and some had been in ministry as deaconesses and then deacons for many years. It was a great privilege to be on this retreat with Sylvia Martin, my old Religious Education teacher, who had nurtured me along that stretch of my spiritual journey when I was at school. She was an early mentor of mine, and the only role model of a female minister I ever had. It was deeply moving for me to be with her on the eve of both our ordination services. Many women had been faithful servants of God in the church for a long time. They hardly dared to believe that priesthood for women might happen in their lifetime, and now some of them at least were to see the "promised land."

IT WAS IN THOSE early years of growth and change that I grew to be good friends with Gordon, who I'd met that first day in the St. Luke's choir. He and I were involved in most church events, were always in the same social circles, and enjoyed playing tennis together. Gordon's dad had died when he was just a little boy, and his mum was a good friend of my parents. On a few occasions our families even went on vacation together.

My friendship with Gordon was unusual and special. We were never romantically involved but became very close friends. We were rather like sister and brother. One minute we would be fighting like cat and dog, and the next minute laughing until we cried. As a teenager my impatience, selfishness, and bad temper often got the better of me, and more often than not, Gordon bore the brunt of it. But he was a true friend who I felt knew and understood the real me. There was none of the mask-wearing or the need to make a good impression as was sometimes the case with boyfriends who came and went.

I was always thankful to have a friend like Gordon, but never more so than after my school day-trip to France. We were so excited — I was fifteen. My school was all girls, and we were being let loose on Boulogne for the day. As we crossed the channel on the ferry, our French teacher handed out worksheets with questions about Boulogne and French culture — in French. It was to be an educational trip. "I want you to spend the day in groups of four or five following the map and finding the answers to my questions. When we meet back at the ferry at 3:00 p.m. I will collect your worksheets." We piled off the ferry and formed into our groups. My friends were like me — not at all interested in the worksheets and very interested in having a good time. What luck! No sooner had we walked fifty yards than there was a group of French boys smiling at us and saying "Bonjour." We looked at each other and grinned. Here was our opportunity to get some help with our worksheets. "Bonjour," we smiled in return, and began to make friends. The French boys were only too happy to provide the answers to our French questions in return for our company for the day. A fair exchange, we thought.

We trailed around Boulogne with these boys practicing our French and they their English. As the day wore on we paired off, held hands, and felt very wicked. Mine was called Marc. Back at the ferry, we kissed our French boyfriends goodbye, and this is where I made my big mistake. I agreed to give Marc my address.

Several weeks passed and the half-term vacation week was approaching. It was a sunny Saturday morning, and Mum and I were going to Croydon shopping center to buy new shoes for me. The mailbox clanked, and a pile of letters fell to the floor. One was a blue airmail letter addressed to me. It was from Marc. Basically it said, "I would like to come and visit you for a week beginning Saturday the 12th. If I don't hear from you I will assume this is okay." As I read the letter open-mouthed, I realized with horror that today was in fact Saturday the 12th.

"Oh, Mum, he won't come will he? I can't believe this. I don't want to look after a French boy all week!" I groaned very loudly and went into denial. "Let's just go shopping and hope he doesn't turn up." When we returned, Marc was on the doorstep with his bag. What followed felt like the worst week of my teenage life! He was a lot less appealing to me than he had been on our day-trip to France. I couldn't imagine that I had even liked him, let alone kissed him!

I took Marc to Superlukes in the crypt that night and introduced him to my friends. I was so embarrassed by my visitor and really annoyed that he would be hanging around with me all through the vacation. Gordon, however, was great. He teased me incessantly and eventually had us all laughing about the situation. Gordon decided that the week needed to be a "show Froggy Marc around London" week. So our gang all bought bus passes and spent the week as tourists. The time passed much too slowly for my liking, but finally the next Saturday arrived. It was time for Marc to go home. At last I was free of him! We took him to the station to catch a train to Dover. The ferry would take him from there back to France. As we waved goodbye on the platform, I breathed such a sigh of relief.

That night I went down to the crypt for Superlukes and began to celebrate with Gordon and my friends. "Thank goodness he's gone," I cried. "Thanks everyone for helping me entertain him. I'm really grateful to you." Gordon put his arm around my shoulder and said, "Joy, don't look now, but I think that's Marc coming down the steps." I swung around and there he was. "No ferry. Too much wind," he said. We all laughed and welcomed him back like an old friend. The next day he really did leave. I learned a lot of lessons from that experience — and one was not to give away too much information on your first date!

Gordon continued to be a good friend as we grew up together; even when I went out with one of his best mates, Brad. Brad's dad was the chaplain at Brixton prison, and his family attended our church. My relationships always seemed to be remarkable in some way, and this was no exception. Soon after Brad and I started going out, he

got knocked over by a double-decker bus. Our relationship consisted mostly of me visiting him in the hospital.
He wrote me beautiful love letters in his despair, and we
would sneak kisses when the nurses weren't looking. The
love thing didn't last long, but we remained friends.

Being a vicar's teenage daughter was an interesting experience. I was often reckless and impulsive. My parents
never expected that I should set a special example simply
because my dad was the local vicar. They did, however,
go through the usual agonies of raising a challenging and
sometimes defiant teenager.

A favorite place to go in the summer months was
Brockwell Park Lido. It was the nearest outdoor public
pool to our school. Whenever it was warm and sunny,
my friends, Sharon and Melanie, and I would go there
straight after school. Sometimes, if the timetable allowed,
we would play truant and skip school to get more hours
in the sun. It was also a great place to meet boys!

There was one particular group of boys that we got to
know over time. One day we all left at the same time and,
to our surprise, they got on the same bus as we did. Not
only that, but then they got off at the same stop as we did.
It turned out that we all lived really close to each other
in West Norwood. And so we became friends with Gary,
"Dougle," and Martin. Martin's family was Catholic, and
he had eight brothers. They were all good-looking and we
girls went through various phases of having crushes on
most of them.

The boys all lived in flats on the York Hill estate, and
it became a regular place to hang out. I started going out
with Gary, and, after our first date, he walked me home. I
hadn't told him what my dad did for a living. We turned
into Chatsworth Way and walked down the street. "This

is it," I said, stopping outside the rather large vicarage. I felt embarrassed, knowing how small Gary's flat was. "Wow. This is a big place," said Gary as he sat on the fence and put his arm around me. "It's not actually ours. It kind of comes with the job," I said hesitantly. "What job is that?" asked Gary. "My dad is the vicar," I replied. At that moment Gary completely lost his balance and fell backwards off the fence into the bushes of the front yard! I hadn't expected him to be quite so shocked. But I was glad to discover that, after the initial surprise and the inevitable vicar's daughter jokes, my new friends accepted me as a person in my own right and never treated me any differently because my dad was a vicar.

As a family, we all enjoyed tennis and belonged to West Norwood Tennis Club. As well as playing regular tennis there, we enjoyed the social club and events laid on for members. During the Wimbledon championships, I would go with friends after school, pay the ground-entrance fee, and hang around the exits of Center Court. Often people who had been at the matches all afternoon would leave at around 5:00 p.m. We would sweetly ask them if they had finished with their tickets before they could drop them in the box to be resold. Almost every time, we got great seats, watching wonderful tennis for hours until the light failed and play stopped for the night.

There were several really good players at our local tennis club. One was a young man named Ray, whom I loved to watch. He played well and looked good. Ray had been tipped to play at Wimbledon some day and had already won many lesser tournaments. Needless to say, he was my tennis-club hero. He was older than me and I mostly admired him from afar but, whenever he took the time to talk to me, I was in seventh heaven. One day, to my surprise and delight, he suggested a double date. He and his friend Rob would take my friend Melanie and me out for a meal in a restaurant.

Melanie was one of my best friends, and we had been through a lot together. The year before, when we were fourteen, her parents had taken me along on their family vacation in Cornwall. One day, while we were swimming in the sea at Duckpool Beach, a freak current, which turned up only once every fifteen years, swept us away. As we were thrown around on rocks and dragged underwater by the raging riptide, we grew more and more terrified. Grown men around us were screaming for their lives. Finally someone on the beach realized that this was a group in trouble, not just having fun a long way from shore. The rescue service was dispatched and soon we heard helicopters overhead. At the same time, lifeguards were coming out with ropes to pull us in. While the helicopters winched some to safety, we were pulled to shore by the lifeguards with ropes. They laid us on the sand and went back for more. The horror of what had just happened began to dawn on us as we looked down at our bodies, which were covered in blood. The fierce waves had thrown us against the rocks so many times that we had hundreds of superficial cuts and scrapes. We were in shock. As we were wrapped up in blankets and given hot tea, newspaper reporters asked us about what had just happened. The next day London's *Evening News* carried the story with the headline: "London Girls Saved in Holiday Drama."

On the night of our double date, we were both really excited. We were only fifteen and had never been taken out for a meal by anyone other than our parents. My parents were less excited. Dad thought Ray was an irresponsible young man and, whenever he disapproved of my friends, he would put greater restrictions on the outing. He wanted me home "no later than 10:30 p.m. Is that clear?" "Yes," I replied, and Melanie and I grinned at each other.

Ray drove a car, and so we felt very grown up driving out to Bromley for a meal. The restaurant there was atmospheric and the food was good, but I quickly realized that Rob was much more interested in Melanie than Ray was in me. "Oh, well, you win some, you lose some," I thought to myself. When the meal was over and the bill paid, we headed back to the parking lot. "We'll just about make it home by 10:30 p.m.," I quickly calculated. It had been a really fun evening. As we drove down a long country lane, the car suddenly began to bump up and down on one side. "Oh, no," exclaimed Ray, "we've got a flat tire."

It took a long time for Ray and Rob to change the wheel. Mel and I looked anxiously at our watches. We would be about half an hour late. They lowered the changed wheel with the jack and looked aghast when it too turned out to be flat. "Now what do we do?" I began to panic — it was, of course, long before the days of mobile phones. "We'll just have to walk until we find a phone booth to call a cab." Which is just what we did. After Ray called the cab, I called my dad. We were already about an hour late and when I said, "Hello, Dad . . . we've got a flat tire," he was not at all pleased. The ride home was tense because I knew I would be in trouble, but I wasn't expecting the reception we got. As the cab pulled up outside our house, Dad came racing up to the car, shaking his fists at

Ray. "What time do you call this? You think I'm stupid enough to believe you had a flat tire?"

"But, Dad..." I tried to interject desperately. "If you think you're ever going out with my daughter again you're very much mistaken!"

I was so embarrassed. I ran inside the house and dissolved into tears. "How could you?" I wailed. It might not have felt so bad if Ray had wanted to go out with me, but actually he didn't, and I felt like a silly young girl with an irate and unreasonable father. How humiliating! I didn't speak to my dad for days and swore that I would never marry a vicar, which was probably the next best thing to saying, "I'm going to get as far away from this kind of restrictive life as I can."

Chapter Three

Ruined for Life

Because my brother, Ray, and I grew up in such an open house, there were always visitors around. They visited from around the country and around the world, coming and going on a regular basis, and we loved to listen to their stories. I especially liked to hear from the missionaries serving God in exotic lands far away, working courageously with the poor of developing countries. One such missionary was George Middleton. He and his Canadian family had been thrown out of Ethiopia when the Communists took control of the country. They went back to Canada with nothing but the clothes on their backs — and a vision. The vision was to train teams of young people to work alongside local churches in developing countries. These teams would bring practical and spiritual help to communities that requested it. In 1975, George Middleton founded Emmanuel International for just that purpose.

In 1977, I was studying for my "A" Levels in the upper-sixth form at St. Martin's. My subjects were English and Religious Studies, and I had been offered a provisional place at the teacher training college of St. Mark and St. John in Plymouth, Devon. I had never really enjoyed

academic work and, in class, my thoughts often wandered
to what I would do when I finished school. I wanted to
defer my college placement and take a year off before
further study. I had heard of young people doing short-
term service overseas but doubted anyone would take
someone with no qualifications like myself. I kept thinking about Emmanuel International. It suddenly struck me
that I might be able to help out for a year at the mission
headquarters in Canada.

"Dear George," I wrote. "I plan to take a year off in
between school and college and I wondered if you could
use me at the mission. I could do anything — even scrub
floors. What do you think?"

George wrote back quickly. He assured me that they
could definitely use me at the mission, but not scrub-
bing floors. He wanted me to join a team that was to
work in Haiti, and training would start in January 1978.
Haiti was the poorest country in the Western hemisphere.
The team was to work with local groups doing relief and
rehabilitation projects.

This was an entirely new proposition. It would mean
leaving school in the middle of my final "A" Level
year and postponing taking exams until I came back.
I would have to get a travel visa and raise money. It
was complicated, but I desperately wanted to do it. My
seventeen-year-old sense of calling was based on the solid
gut feeling that I absolutely had to do this — whatever the
obstacles.

The first obstacles were my parents. Reluctant to let
their little girl loose on this adventure into the unknown,
they felt sure that it couldn't possibly work for me. "If
it turns out not to be possible, I'll let it go," I said, "but
let's at least try." I was ironing. I put the iron firmly down

on the board and looked them in the eye, "Mum, Dad, I have never felt so sure about anything in my whole life."

My parents finally gave me their blessing, agreeing to help. Privately, they were certain that the headmistress at my school would not allow me to postpone my "A" Levels and that would be that. We went to see her together. After listening to my plan, she thought it was an excellent idea and offered to arrange for me to take my exams a year later than scheduled. My parents were shocked at her flexibility, and Dad wondered aloud if she was simply pleased at the opportunity to get rid of me!

It took a while to get a visa but, with that done, I moved ahead with travel plans. Freddie Laker's Sky Train was in business and upsetting other airlines with very cheap fares from London to New York. Even though it meant lining up on the morning of travel to buy the ticket, it was a great deal. I then needed a connecting flight on another airline from New York to Toronto. When our travel agent tried to book the reservation, he found that many airlines were boycotting passengers who were traveling on Sky Train and refused to book my connecting flight. My dad sprang into action. He called a leading Canadian airline from home and booked the ticket from New York to Toronto. When they asked him, "How is your daughter getting to New York?" He replied, "She's swimming!" It was none of their business how I was traveling to New York, and they had no choice but to sell me a ticket. On the morning I was to travel, I woke up with a dreadful toothache. After lining up at the crack of dawn for my Sky Train ticket, I went to have a molar extracted. My family and best friends came to see me off on my adventure.

I arrived in New York during an ice storm. The doors on the plane were frozen shut. The delay caused by the time it took to thaw the doors meant that I missed my connecting flight to Toronto. It was the last flight out that day and I had to spend the night, scared and alone with my luggage, in New York's JFK Airport. At six o'clock the next morning, tired but happy not to have been mugged, I was finally on my way to Emmanuel's training school in Stouffville, Ontario, just outside Toronto.

Emmanuel International has a reputation for seeing the potential in young people and helping them to grow. It trained young people that no other mission organization would take — and I was one of them. Like me, the young people who came often had no college training or degree. We had no particular skills, just a fire in the belly and lots of enthusiasm.

A thick blanket of snow covered the countryside around the Canadian mission. As the snow often fell silently outside, we gathered each day around a warm fireplace for training school. Cultural orientation, spirituality, team-building, relationships, and rehabilitation projects were some of our lessons. But it was outside the classroom that the most effective formation took place.

One particularly cold afternoon, George Middleton announced that someone had kindly donated a truck to the mission and that he had to go to Orillia to pick it up. "Joy," he said, "I'd like you to come with me to get the truck, then follow me back in the car." "No problem," I replied.

We drove to Orillia, got the truck, and began our journey home in separate vehicles. That is where the problems began. The roads in Orillia are a series of very steep hills. The first had a stop sign perched at the very top. This was followed by a steep hill down before ascending the next hill — with another stop sign at the top. All this would

have been fine if there weren't several inches of snow and
ice covering the roads! As I had only just got my driving
license in England, I had no idea how to drive on snow
and ice, let alone up and down steep hills. Just as I reached
the top of each hill, I'd slow down for the stop sign; then
the car would roll back down the hill and I just couldn't
get it up again.

Close to tears, I got out of the car and told George
that I simply couldn't do it. He gently, but firmly, told
me to get back in the car and try again. At least five times
George implored me to get back in the car. Finally I ended
up with the nose of the car in a snow bank off the side of
the road. "Please, George," I wailed, "get someone else to
come and get us. I can't do this!" George said, "Joy, get
back in the car and try again." This time, after we pushed
and pulled the car back onto the road, I finally got it. Up
and down each hill we went, my confidence growing with
each one we conquered. I learned how to drive in snow
and ice that day, but I also learned about not giving up.
I learned to keep trying even when something seems im-
possibly difficult. At eighteen years old, these were good
lessons to learn.

There were also lessons in love. I met Dave, a Canadian
policeman, at church. He lived with his parents and was
just starting his policing career. He was a good-looking
guy and drove a big motorbike. He often drove the fifty
miles from his home in Mississauga to pick me up for
the weekend. I was completely swept off my feet, and we
began to talk about getting married. When my parents
and brother came to visit me in Canada, Dave took the
opportunity to ask my dad's permission to marry me. I
decided that I would put off such a big decision until after

I returned from Haiti. Instead of an engagement ring, I went to Haiti with a "promise ring."

It was a cool May morning when our team of four climbed into the beat-up old minivan that was to take us to Miami, where we would connect to our flight to Port au Prince. My mum, dad, brother, Ray, and Dave were there to see us off.

Our team consisted of myself, an American, an Ethiopian, and a Canadian. Mark Middleton, George's son, was soon to become the director of Emmanuel International. It was his job to drive us from Stouffville, Ontario, to Miami. Churches offered us hospitality along the way, and, in return, we spoke at their meetings and services about our mission. When we finally arrived in Miami, our training finished and Mark waving goodbye, I was terrified. What had I got myself into? All I could do was trust that God had guided me to this place and that I had made the right decisions at each juncture. I was full of doubt and unsure how I would cope. We flew with a missionary airline to Haiti on a DC-3, aptly nicknamed "the vomit comet."

In Haiti, the heat wrapped itself around me like a hot blanket. Dust blew up from the dirt roads. As we passed through villages, small children leapt up onto the vehicle in glee to greet their white visitors. Chickens, hogs, and dogs roamed the streets looking for scraps of rubbish to eat. Donkeys were the main mode of transport. Men and women sat by the roadside selling their wares, including watermelons, mangos, bananas, and citrons. After several hours we arrived at our destination in St. Marc. The local church and missionaries served us the best-tasting iced tea I ever remember drinking. I was so thirsty that it felt as though I was drinking the life back into my body.

The house in St. Marc was empty when we arrived. There was no electricity, no running water, no mosquito screens, and one outdoor toilet swarming with flies. For days and weeks, all I did was clean the house, trying to make the place habitable. Soon the work on the house was complete, the electricity and running water were hooked up, and we had a decent bathroom — thank God. Our neighbor was a pig breeder of sorts, and the smell was horrible; I have never been able to enjoy ham since!

Our first few months in Haiti were frustrating. Much of our work was with a mobile health clinic. The clinic was held up in Haitian customs, as they were waiting for a bribe to get it out. In the meantime, we were busy tapping springs for wells and digging latrines. I spent time with a women's Bible-study group and ran a summer vacation project for children in the village. One day, when the temperature was well over a hundred degrees, we helped to build a roof on a new school. I fainted in the heat and had to be lifted off the roof in the bulldozer bucket!

Finally our mobile clinic was cleared through customs, and we ventured into remote villages with a Haitian doctor and nurse. Sometimes the villages we visited were far up a deserted mountain track or separated from us by a deep river. Then we loaded the supplies onto donkeys and saddle bags and waded across waist-deep rivers. The reception when we arrived at the remote village made it all worthwhile. People needed the basics such as vitamins, antiseptic ointments, aspirin, eye drops, and vaccinations. I'd never given an injection before but, after a few lessons using an orange, I took up the job. When it was too late to make the journey home, we would stay the night with families in the village. I remember the first time I had chicken soup made from the whole chicken. It would have been rude not to eat the chicken heart, so I washed it down with a big swallow of evaporated milk and beetroot juice!

In Haiti I saw things that troubled me. I was not only dealing with Haitian culture shock but, as an Anglican, I was also dealing with American Baptist shock. It worried me that the Christian churches in Haiti were like American churches. The hymns were American hymns translated into Creole. In every respect, except language, the services were American. When the Haitians converted to Christianity, they were expected to renounce their past completely because of the strong influence of voodoo in the culture. They were encouraged to burn their possessions and leave their family; it was a conversion to American culture as well as to Christianity. There was no sense in which the Haitian culture could be converted or redeemed.

Garth Hewitt, a Christian musician committed to the poor, had been to Haiti a few months earlier. His music had a good beat and his gospel concert had the place rocking. The Haitians loved it, but many of the American missionaries hated it. They considered it to be spiritually compromising for Haitian Christians. They thought that any drumbeat was too closely connected with the voodoo drums to be spiritually edifying. Thus began for me a lifetime of theological questions that have never stopped. I came out of Haiti not only with new questions but also with new values. I was determined to do something with my life that made a difference to other people's lives.

Unfortunately, my relationship with Dave didn't survive all the changes taking place in me. I now knew my future was not to be a suburban policeman's wife and that the next step was to get qualifications to be a teacher in England.

After living with some of the poorest people on earth, I was — to use the phrase coined by the American Jesuit Volunteer Corps — "ruined for life." Something got into my blood as an eighteen-year-old in Haiti that has never gone away. I became sensitized to the plight of people at the bottom of society — those left behind or shut out. My life's work, particularly as a priest, was set in place because of Haiti. In January 1979, I went home to take my "A" Level exams and took the next giant step to teacher-training college.

"WALKING ON THE MOON," by The Police, was playing while I danced at the college disco. I was in the middle of my first term at the College of St. Mark and St. John, or "Marjons," in Devon. I had chosen a college that was a long way from home and was enjoying my independence.

Marjons specialized in the training of physical education teachers, and the campus, well outside the city of Plymouth, boasted a number of playing fields and rugby pitches. It was only a short drive to the rugged and beautiful Dartmoor, where sheep grazed alongside wild ponies amid heather and the ancient tors. Life was an adventure; I was an adult with my life to live. No longer did my parents need to know where I was, whom I was with, or what time I would be home. Now I had to think and speak for myself. These felt like giant steps, and I was happy to take them.

I jumped in the air as I danced at the disco that night, but landed badly on my foot. I literally came to earth with a bump and hobbled to my room for a good night's sleep. I was taking part in my first protest march the next morning against Margaret Thatcher's education cuts. I had thrown

Too much dancing and protest marching –
with my broken foot at the College of St. Mark
and St. John, Plymouth, 1979.

myself into Student Union politics and was angry about
Thatcherite education policies.

I awoke to the alarm with a throbbing ankle. Determined not to miss the march, I bandaged up my foot,
wedged it into an unlaced running shoe, and took some
painkillers. I helped carry a banner, which read "Maggie
Thatcher, Right Snatcher," the seven miles into Plymouth
city center. The rally was a great success. However, there
was increasing pain in my foot, so I continued my march
straight into the emergency room of the city hospital.
After an examination and an X-ray, I emerged in a
wheelchair with my leg in plaster up to the knee. Between
dancing and protesting, I had broken a bone in my foot,
and now my education curriculum included how to use a
pair of crutches!

Thus began what Ray called my "socialist phase." My
experiences in both Haiti and teacher training college did
a lot to shape my social values. When Richard Curtis
wrote *The Vicar of Dibley*, it pleased me greatly that both
my concern for the poor and my passion for social justice
were translated into major themes in the show.

At college, I was much more interested in the Student Union than the Christian Union. It was only on rare occasions that I attended chapel services. The chaplain knew I was a Christian and the daughter of a vicar but never made me feel guilty for being so inactive and uncommitted to the Marjons worshiping community. He recognized my need to do my own thing and distance myself from the religious practices I had grown up with. At college I went through a spiritual rebellion. While I always professed to be a Christian and didn't doubt God, I didn't do much about it in terms of religious practice.

My dad often described church as a burning coal fire. Together the coals burn brightly and give out warmth and light, but if one piece of coal is isolated on the hearth it will burn out and go cold. Perhaps I wanted to test the theory. I didn't quite burn out, but it wasn't until I moved back to London and became an active member of a local church that I generated any spiritual heat.

Political heat was another thing altogether. I did what was required of me academically, but most of my energy went into student politics and having fun. I served on the Union Executive and spent a disproportionate amount of time in the college bar, singing songs with the Marjon rugby team that were hardly fitting for a future priest. As it turned out, one of the lads on the rugby team also eventually became a priest in Wales. Neither of us was a likely candidate at the time. No one sitting in that rugby circle could have predicted that we would be ordained, but he, too, was the offspring of a clergyman.

It was at college that I owned my first car — a navy blue, box-shaped Vauxhall Viva. It cost me fifty pounds, and I loved it. With the help of a Greek family friend and car mechanic, Nick, it made many trips from London to Plymouth and back again. I became rather good at basic car maintenance and roadside repairs. I changed tires and even repaired split hoses. I once made a very temporary repair using rubber bands and clothes pins in the engine, and just about made it home. The license plate was unique, and my dad quickly pointed out that it was better than a personalized plate. The first three letters were COW. Needless to say, I was very fond of the old "Cow."

One night I loaned my car to a friend. Whenever I parked it beside the house, I always left it in first gear, as the hand brake didn't work very well, and I lived on a hill. I must have forgotten to tell my friend about the hand brake. When he returned my car that night, he parked it in its usual place. When I got up the next morning, I was surprised that it wasn't there. Perhaps he parked it somewhere else, I thought. Upon closer inspection, I saw tire marks on the grass.

I frantically began to follow the tracks down the grassy hill. I increased to a run when I saw a flattened fir tree. What else had the car taken out on its driverless journey? At the bottom of the hill, the fence had been completely flattened about ten feet across. Beyond the fence was the duck pond. At the water's edge, I saw my beloved car hood down in the pond — just the trunk and two back wheels stuck up out of the water, with the license plate for all to see.

At the office of the campus groundskeepers I knocked on the door. "Look, I'm terribly sorry, but my car is in the middle of the campus duck pond." They looked at me as if to say, what kind of wild time did you have last night? Fortunately, they towed it out with a tractor, but not before a small crowd of students had gathered to laugh.

The "Cow" went to car heaven, but I kept the license plate as a memento. Mounted, with a poem written by my dad on the back, it still hangs in my house. The little limerick reads:

> There was once a silly old cow
> Who had to stay on a hill's brow.
> She had a great thirst
> And descended head first
> to the mud of the pond like a sow.

While I was at college, my parents moved to Purley in Surrey, where Dad was installed as the vicar of Christ Church in 1981. I graduated in the summer of 1982 with a Bachelor of Education degree and found a temporary job for the summer at Gatwick Airport. With only a twenty-minute drive to Gatwick from Purley, it was the ideal place to live while I worked at the airport. It felt strange to be staying with my parents in their new home — it didn't feel like my home any more. Gone was my old bedroom and gone was the old neighborhood. Life had moved on and I had become an adult.

It was fun to work for British Caledonian as a ground stewardess. After a period of training, I was assigned to departing and incoming flights, which included the unpleasant task of dealing with customers who had lost their baggage. It's true that many people seem to leave their brains behind when they enter the doors of an airport, and I came home every day with stories that made Mum and Dad laugh. A woman came up to me one day in the baggage hall and said, "Excuse me, my bag is missing." "Who are you traveling with?" I asked, wanting to direct her to the correct airline agent. "My husband," she replied.

I wore a red tartan uniform, complete with cute hat, and for four months was able to live out one of my little-girl fantasies to be an airline stewardess. The novelty soon wore off. I worked shifts — four days on and three days off — and was up for the early shift at 4:00 a.m., so hardly ever saw my friends. It was a fabulous summer job but I was looking forward to finding a job as a teacher in the autumn.

Chapter Four

The Calling

"Surprise! How was your trip?" We hugged. Gordon looked at me and smiled. "It was great. All the better for being met by you!" Gordon had become a travel agent. He had begun to do well and was traveling a lot himself. It was July 1982 and I knew that he was flying in to Gatwick, returning from his first visit to America. I was still working at Gatwick and was on duty that day.

I noticed he looked a little pale. "Are you feeling okay?"

"Well actually," he said, "I've got a dreadful headache. I think I'm going to go straight home to bed."

I took his arm and we walked back through passport control and on to collect his luggage. "You go home, take some pain-killers, and I'll phone you later."

The next time I saw Gordon, he was in King's College Hospital. That night when he'd got home, he'd had a massive seizure caused by a brain tumor. The tumor was too big and too deep to operate. Chemotherapy was the only course of action, and the chances of survival were extremely slim. I couldn't believe it. "How dreadful for a mother to lose her beloved son. And for me," I thought selfishly, "I have to lose my best friend at the age of twenty-three. This is not fair."

That night I stood in the shower for more than an hour and sobbed for his mum, for his brother, for myself, for all Gordon's friends, and for him and the life that he might not get to live. I sobbed for the children he wouldn't have, the goals he wouldn't reach, and even the tears he wouldn't cry. What a waste. I was suddenly aware of the fragility of life for the first time. No one close to me had ever been ill enough to die, and now it was all too real. I felt numb and weak. I simply stood there as the water cascaded down my body and felt the painful ache of something very important being ripped away. I felt cheated. I wailed at God over the big question that is still so hard to answer: "Why?"

Gordon's hospital room was constantly full of family and friends coming and going. The flow of conversation and banter was regular and upbeat. It was almost as if the cancer would go away if no one ever talked about it. I often felt frustrated and wondered if anyone would ever talk to Gordon about dying. How could we help him be ready and not too afraid? But none of us really knew what to say.

As the months of vigil slowly passed by I looked for opportunities to be alone with Gordon, but they never came. For a few short weeks, he was allowed to come home. He was confined to a wheelchair, but his mates made sure he got to the pub. The Hornes Tavern was full of friends who turned out to welcome Gordon back. Unfortunately, his time at home was cut short when he suffered another seizure and was returned to the hospital. This time Gordon was very weak and often incoherent.

The stream of visitors slowed down, and I found a few moments now and then when I could simply hold Gordon's hand and gently talk, not really knowing if he could hear. "You're safe. You're loved. Don't be afraid. There's something better ahead. Jesus is walking this journey with you." Inside, I was full of doubt and my private prayers were more like, "God, I hope you exist because right now I'm not sure. I don't know where Gordon's going, but if you are real, please take him through this passage without fear."

The new vicar at St. Luke's visited Gordon regularly, and one night he called me on the phone. "Joy, I've been with Gordon for a while and he's been totally incoherent until just now when he asked for you. Can you come?" "Of course," I replied. I spent the rest of that evening with Gordon until he slept.

Even though a two-way conversation with Gordon was just about impossible, I would visit and tell him my news. In November, I was very proud to be able to tell him that, at last, I had got my first job as a teacher. I knew he would be pleased for me.

Robert Straker, the headmaster at St. Luke's Church of England Primary School, had given me a temporary teaching position. I handed in my resignation at British Caledonian and became the teacher to the top class of eleven-year-olds. They were a wild bunch. I was their second teacher that year and they were not about to cut me any slack for being brand new. I was thrown in at the deep end and, at the end of each horrible day, Robert would say to me something that felt like, "Just keep swimming!" This was the man who later placed a five-pound bet at Ladbroke's that I would be the first woman bishop in England!

British Caledonian girl:
my summer job in 1982.

The school bell rang. It was 3:30 p.m., at the end of another tough week in December. The kids noisily left the classroom, eager to get home for the weekend. Robert walked in. "Joy, why don't you sit down?"

"Oh, I'm okay. Just another week in the life of..." I sighed smiling.

Robert didn't smile back and said again, "Joy, sit down." I sat. I wondered what I had done wrong. Shouting too much? Perhaps he was about to tell me I wasn't cut out to be a teacher. "Joy," he said gently, "Gordon died today."

On Friday, December 10, 1982, Gordon was buried in West Norwood Cemetery next to his dad. The chapel was full to bursting as my dad conducted the funeral, giving thanks to God for Gordon's too-brief life. My memory of the service is a teary blur. As we stood around the gaping hole in the muddy ground, someone reached into the enormous bank of wreaths and flowers, picked up a rose, and threw it on top of the coffin as it was lowered. It was over. In the days that followed, I cried easily and simply missed Gordon terribly. Our friendship was one that I imagine would have changed and lasted through the years, and I grieved the loss of that.

Any time I felt sad or missed Gordon, I would walk through the cemetery, find his grave, and sit with my notebook. I would write down my thoughts as if I were writing to him. "Dear Gordon, I thought about you a lot yesterday when I met Tracey's new boyfriend. I tried to imagine what you would have thought of him. I still miss you but it's not as painful as it was a month ago. . . . "

After about six months, I no longer felt the need to write to Gordon, but I did continue to keep a journal. My journal writing led me to explore my feelings about God and my life. Suddenly I was in touch with a part of myself that had been neglected: I suppose it was my spirituality. I began to really think through what I believed, why I believed it, and, more importantly, what I didn't believe. I struggled with doubts and grappled with the concept of "meaning" in my life. I questioned some of the evangelical teachings that I had grown up with and began to work on a rationale for Christianity that made sense in my life.

I believed in God, a mighty creator. It was impossible for me to look at the intricacy of creation and not believe that some power greater than ourselves was behind it all. Someone once said that there was as much chance of the world randomly falling together as a result of the Big Bang as there was of a dictionary falling together after an explosion in a print factory. At the same time, I didn't believe that the Genesis story of creation was a literal account of how God created the universe. It seemed obvious to me that these were stories inspired by God to explain that God did indeed create the world, but were never intended to be a scientific description of how it was done.

I believed in the person of Jesus Christ as God made human in the world. Jesus was always a radical figure to me. He appealed to my rebellious nature, turning tables and people's lives upside down. He stood up for the weak, the poor, the powerless, and the outcast, and he refused to pay homage to the rulers and religious leaders who oppressed them. I chose to accept his claim to be God and was blown away by the idea that God chose to enter into the history of the world at a particular time and in the form of a real person. I later learned that this was known as the incarnation and it has always been central to my faith in a God who identifies with our brokenness and vulnerability — our humanity in all its expressions.

It was Jesus who also made Christianity different from other religions I had heard about, because through Jesus redemption was possible. It seems clear to me that we human beings can never hope to get anywhere close to perfection and somehow need to be accepted, warts, and all. The imagery of Christ as the sacrificial lamb who was the ultimate sacrifice that made us acceptable to God — even though we are so often very unacceptable — provided me with a notion of hope when all seems hopeless. And so the cross as the place of Jesus' death and the empty tomb as the evidence of his resurrection were also vital in my belief system. As I grew in understanding, it became obvious why Christmas and Easter were the two most important holy days for the church. All else finds its place in Christianity in relation to the incarnation and the resurrection.

Finally, I believed in a living God. It was important to me that it didn't all end when Jesus disappeared back into heaven. The living essence, the spirit of God, was given to the followers of Jesus, those left behind to found and be the church. The spirit of God is the fuel for the Christian journey. Spiritual gifts from God equip the church — the people — to serve and be the hands and feet of Jesus in the world.

These were my core beliefs, and I can't remember a time when I didn't believe them. I believed the Bible to be the inspired word of God but had serious questions about how it was often interpreted. I often disagreed with the teachings of some conservative evangelical clergy and didn't hesitate to say so. I disliked what I perceived as an evangelical lust for certainty, when I was just beginning to explore the diversity and the mystery of God. I began to realize how unhelpful the old labels were as I tried to define what kind of Christian I was.

Much of these early explorations of God and spirituality took place at Gordon's grave and in the aftermath of his death. Two years later, I was talking to the bishop of Southwark about the possibility of training to be a minister in the church. The death of my friend was a significant milestone in my spiritual journey that was to lead eventually to ordination.

Being a teacher was one of the great loves of my life. I now had a class of thirty five- and six-year-olds at Gonville Primary School in Thornton Heath, South London. Half the class stayed with me for two years and, when the new children arrived to start school, the ones who had been with me for a year already were able to help the newcomers settle in. It was a demanding job.

My years as a teacher were rewarding, and the kids were a wonderful bunch.
A number of them surprised me in church, ten years later, with a reunion.

With children of different ages and abilities working together, the topics and tasks had to provide each one of
them with the appropriate learning experience. The key
was to be organized. I usually stayed late after school,
preparing the children's work for the next day, and would
arrive early enough in the morning to be ready as the
parents delivered their little ones.

"Miss Carroll, Miss Carroll! Look what I've brought
in to show the class."

"Miss Carroll, I went to my grandma's house last night
and..."

"Miss Carroll..."

Thirty little voices would chatter excitedly on the carpet
as they sat around my feet. When I had taken the roll, we
would walk quietly to the hall for the morning assembly.
The school was not a church school and was situated in

a predominantly Asian neighborhood. Many of the children were Hindu or Muslim, and so our assemblies were not overtly Christian in nature. God was experienced in different ways by this diverse gathering of children, and our role was to help them to understand and be tolerant of each other's religions. Easter was explained with as much care as Diwali. I played the guitar and, when I introduced a new religious song to my class or the school, I often had to change the words to enable everyone to join in with integrity. In one particular song, for example, I changed the word "Father" to "God." A generic "God" replaced a traditionally Christian understanding of God as "Father."

The mornings were always hectic. As the children settled down to their work, I would listen to individual children reading to me. This was so important, especially for the children for whom English was a second language at home. I tried to hear each child several times a week, which was never easy while having to respond to the needs of other children at the same time. I will never forget one pupil, James, who often wanted my attention and was unwilling to share me with anyone else. If I was talking to another child when he needed me, he would put his hand across my cheek, pull my face toward his and say firmly, "Miss Carroll, I *need* you!"

I loved my job and worked very hard at it. On Friday evenings I kept my diary clear as I almost always went to bed with a migraine. It was as though tension built up throughout the week and then, when I switched off on Friday, my body had permission to protest.

I was busy outside school, too. When I first began teaching, money was tight, and so I also worked some evenings as a barmaid in the Irish pub across the street from St. Luke's Church. I got to know the local clientele and learned how to pull the perfect pint of Guinness, complete with a shamrock in the froth on top. When regular customers walked through the door, I'd have their drinks ready before they reached the bar. Like lots of pubs, the Hornes Tavern was for many, especially the elderly, an extension of their living room. It was a warm and friendly local pub where, fortunately for me, a number of my friends gathered too. Looking back on my time as a barmaid, I realize now that I learned a lot of pastoral skills while pouring drinks for the customers.

One night the landlord had gone out and left me and another barman called Colin in charge for the evening. A young man had looked nervous all evening as he drank at the bar, and he was clearly afraid of something. At closing time he didn't want to go home and so he locked himself in the toilet. As we began to clean up and the pub slowly emptied, it became obvious that this guy really was afraid that someone was out to get him and was not leaving. I stood outside the toilet door for about twenty minutes talking to the man, listening to his ramblings, and trying to reassure him. All of a sudden he was quiet. Colin ran outside and climbed up to look in the toilet window. I heard Colin shout, "My God, he's cut his wrists!" We called an ambulance and broke down the door. Colin was trained in first aid, and I did what he told me. I grabbed a pile of tea towels from behind the bar and tied them around his wrists above the cuts.

"Colin," I called, "the blood's still coming out."

"Then press your fingers hard on his wrists to stop the flow, and hold his arms up." I sat with my hands covered in blood, holding up the man's bleeding arms for what seemed like an eternity. My hands were almost numb and my arms aching badly when the ambulance finally arrived. I was definitely not about to give up my day job!

During that time I lived in a little terraced house in Robson Road with my friend Nicola. My dad had bought two houses next door to each other for a song. My brother, Ray, lived in the other one with two of his friends. We had a lot of fun living next door to each other, as well as times when we drove each other crazy. It was a period in life when we were young, single, and relatively carefree.

We used both houses and backyard for great parties. Ray's house was open-plan in design, and it had a great space for dancing. My house was divided into two rooms and was a quieter space where people could talk. People could move between the two houses through the backyards, which were joined together. Fancy-dress parties with themes like "back to school" gave us ample opportunity to be mad, young things. We would walk to the pub for a preparty drink, just to show off our carefully prepared costumes. I lived in a world where God and life were closely entwined. Both the church and pub were the centers of my activity. Did we ever have a "vicars and tarts" party? Well, of course we did — and I went as a vicar. Little did I know that, several years later, I really would be a vicar and would often be asked, "Are you in fancy dress?"

A friendly warfare was continually waged in Robson Road, between the boys' and the girls' houses. One day, after Ray had dropped some leaves into the mailbox, Nicky decided to get her revenge. The World Cup was on, and one of the England matches clashed with a church meeting being held at Ray's house. The boys had decided to record the game and watch it when everyone had gone home. They didn't want to know the score so that they could watch it as if it were live. After the meeting, they settled down on the couch with a beer. Suddenly Nicky appeared outside the glass sliding doors. She was standing in their backyard holding up a big sheet of poster paper with the score written on it.

I once again became an active member of St. Luke's, where my father had been vicar before his move to Purley. I worked as a Sunday School teacher and a member of a house group. I was also a member of the parish visiting team and a regular visitor at a local nursing home, which had the unfortunate name of the British Home for Incurables. As a teenager, I had volunteered at the home on Saturdays. One of my jobs had been to feed a woman who had multiple sclerosis. She had lost control of her whole body and I helped her eat her food and drink through a straw, just as I did when I babysat children. The most difficult part for me was taking her back to her room, where she had photographs all around of herself with her family. Not so long before, she had been a vibrant and healthy woman. Her brain was still perfectly intact and she loved me to talk to her, even though I could barely understand her responses. Having that relationship with someone who had been struck by such a cruel disease affected me deeply as a teenager. I would always go home feeling depressed and, on two occasions, was physically sick. Now, as an adult member of St. Luke's Church, I was glad to have the opportunity once again to go to the British Home for Incurables. I went with a group once a month on a Sunday afternoon, where we led a service in the chapel and visited the patients.

As well as being a place of worship, St. Luke's was very much a social hub. It was around this time that I began to notice a very good-looking young man who appeared at the back of the church every Sunday. He had dark, wavy hair, distinctive brown eyes, and chiseled features that made it very difficult not to notice him. He always arrived after the service had started and left before the distribution of Holy Communion, so it was a long time before I found out who he was. Each Sunday he would stay a little bit longer, until at last he stayed for the whole service. After months of wondering who this handsome stranger was, I took my chance to find out.

"Hi. Welcome to St. Luke's. Won't you stay for coffee?" I held out my hand and he shook it firmly. "My name's Steven, and I moved into West Norwood a few months ago. I've been coming here for a while but couldn't bring myself to stay. I wasn't really ready to meet anyone and get involved."

Steve had just left the army and was recovering from a time in Northern Ireland that had shaken him to the core. A large part of his coming to church was to find peace with God. Steve was now the manager of a sports center in Brixton. He was incredibly fit and a great sportsman. He had a gregarious personality and could spin a yarn that would have me and my friends curled up with laughter. He was soon a firm friend, part of the "gang," and a member of our church.

For a time, Steve and I were a couple. We were both extroverts and spent most of our time together with our other friends. We were also both very opinion-ated and had strong personalities. We had the inevitable arguments, and our relationship was something of a roller-coaster ride. Steve liked to make things happen, which I enjoyed. He organized a vacation for the gang in a converted windmill on the Norfolk Broads, and on the first of January for several years, he hosted a church badminton tournament. However late we had all been up the night before at New Year's Eve parties, we all gathered the next morning to leap around a badminton court in an attempt to win the coveted trophy.

Our relationship didn't last, but our friendship did — just. We had gone through a period where we were always angry with each other. Having been a couple and remaining part of the same crowd, we were still close enough to drive each other mad. The friction between us was never far away, and the sparks flew too often. On the windmill vacation we'd had a row, and now we weren't speaking to each other.

I was watching the local news one lunchtime and could hardly believe my eyes when I saw Steve's picture on the TV screen. The news anchor was telling how Steve had been stabbed by an intruder in his home and was fighting for his life in the hospital. That day he'd had a late start and didn't have to be at the sports center until late morning. At about 10:00 a.m., he'd been in his bathrobe when he'd heard noises in the corridor outside his flat. He'd looked out and found a young man trying to break into another flat in the building. Steve was strong and confident. He tackled the man successfully, holding him securely, then walked him into his own flat and threw him down on the couch. He'd picked up the telephone to call the police when all of a sudden the man lunged at him with a knife and stabbed him three times in the chest. Steve bravely fought him off and eventually the man ran out of the house, slamming the front door shut behind him. Feeling weaker and weaker, Steve held on to the phone, which was now connected to the police station. He just about managed to tell the police what had happened before he collapsed.

A series of miracles saved Steve's life that day. The first was that the police car that received the emergency call just happened to be passing the bottom of Steve's road. The police arrived extremely quickly and broke into the house. Just as amazingly, an ambulance was passing the top of the road and arrived a minute or so after the police had broken in. The ambulance took Steve to the hospital and, on the way, his heart stopped three times. On arrival at emergency room, the senior cardiac surgeon, Dr. Pugsley, just happened to be going off-duty and was able to perform open-heart surgery right there in the emergency room. Steve's attacker had managed to pierce his heart and both his lungs: every second was crucial.

Steve was in such good physical condition that his body was able to cope with the assault, and he healed quickly with no complications. The scars on his otherwise perfect body became a testament to his strength and bravery.

I was shaken beyond belief by the attack. We had almost lost Steve, and the last words he and I had said to each other had been angry ones. How stupid was that? I needed to see Steve and put things right between us. I sat beside his bed and begged him to forgive me. "Steve, I'm so sorry. We shouldn't do this to each other. You mean the world to me. We need to take care of our friendship. It's too precious to be the victim of our tempers and egos."

I had learned a big lesson about myself. I needed to be more careful with my friends and how I treated them. Friendship is precious and life is fragile. Human pride and an unwillingness to forgive can destroy friendships and turn the best of us into sad and bitter people. What a shame that it took such a disaster to make me aware of that.

IN THE SCHOOL SUMMER VACATION, I was one of the leaders who took sixty children to a Christian camp called Pathfinder in Devon for ten days. At the British Home for Incurables and at Pathfinder camp, I was able to practice my skills as a communicator when I was given regular opportunities to preach. It wasn't long before people began to make comments, such as, "Joy, you have a gift. You are able to communicate quite complicated theological concepts in very understandable ways." "Joy, you are a natural organizer and leader." "Joy, have you ever thought about doing full-time Christian work?"

It was because of compliments like these that I started to consider a change of direction in my life. I began to explore a sense of calling to be a minister of some kind. I had a very vague notion that I could contribute in some way to the work of the Christian church, perhaps with youth, perhaps even as a leader, but I had no idea that following that sense of vocation would lead me to become a priest. The whole process was a bit like the negative of a photograph being developed; just as the contents of a photograph gradually become visible, it became clear only over time where my exploration was leading.

I talked to friends at church; I talked it over with Mum and Dad; I talked to Christian leaders outside the Church of England. I had a friend, Clive, who was the director of the Evangelical Alliance. He and his wife, Ruth, had four children and I was their babysitter for a while. For several years at Easter, I also went with them to a Christian teaching event called Spring Harvest to look after the children while they coordinated the event and led seminars.

I trusted and respected Clive's judgment and so shared with him my sense of calling as it unfolded. He asked me some tough questions: "Have you considered that in the

Church of England you are under the authority of the bishop? What if you have a vision or theology different from that of your bishop?" I was forced to think through questions that might have been asked only by noncon- formists who prefer to do church without bishops. Clive also encouraged me and took my exploration seriously. In fact, while I was training at theological college, he took a big risk and invited me to be a speaker at the Spring Harvest event. I was young and not yet qualified as a minister, yet he gave me a chance to gain experience and confidence. I was just starting out and my presentations must have left a lot to be desired, but Clive knew the importance of developing the potential in people. I was very grateful, not only to be given a chance, but also to learn about enabling and encouraging — a very important leadership quality.

It was also important to me that a wide community of people recognized my calling to ministry. It wasn't some- thing that I simply decided to do all by myself. Almost everyone had affirmed my sense of calling, but I was ner- vous. It made sense for me to be a minister in the Church of England as I was Anglican, born and bred. It was the obvious place to offer myself for ministry. And yet this meant that, if I was accepted, I would become a dea- coness. A deaconess — help! I knew of no deaconesses who were young women like me. I definitely did not fit the stereotypical image and was afraid of what I might have to become. The only deaconesses I knew were middle- aged and not at all like me. It was a big step for me to realize that I should and could be myself. It was me God was calling, not someone else who I needed to somehow turn myself into.

"All I can do is try," I thought to myself. "I can offer myself as I am, warts and all, and if the church doesn't want me, then fair enough. I'll know that I wasn't suitable and that will be that." I was ambivalent. There was a part of me that would have been relieved to be turned down by the church. It felt like such a big step of commitment and probable sacrifice, and I needed to be sure I was called to take it. It was hugely comforting to know that it wasn't just up to me. I eventually contacted the bishop's director of ordinands to "test the doors" as we say in the Christian world — and there were to be a lot of them. The selection procedure in the Church of England involves a lot of people and a number of interviews with the appropriate diocesan officials. The job of the director of ordinands was to work with people like me in determining whether a sense of calling should be put before a selection conference.

I was home one Saturday morning when I got a call from the vicar of St. Luke's. "Joy, I've had a letter from the bishop's office asking me to write a reference for you as part of the discernment process, and I'd like to come and talk to you about it." The vicar was on his way round and I put the kettle on. "I wonder what it is he wants to talk about?" I thought to myself. I knew that selectors were very interested in a candidate's involvement with the church they belonged to, and my vicar's support was obviously important. I also knew that the vicar was a conservative evangelical who was opposed to women being in positions of headship in the church, and I wondered whether he was concerned about my moving toward this.

I was soon to find out. I invited him to sit and we drank our cups of tea. He talked a little about his theological position regarding women in ministry and then said, " ... but quite frankly, Joy, what really concerns me more than anything is the amount of time you spend in the pub." I almost laughed out loud but managed not to.

I replied, "I actually think that it's a good place to spend time. That's where many of the people in our parish can be found and I think that, if Jesus were walking the earth today, he would upset a lot of church leaders by spending a lot of his time with those people in the pub!"

We talked and talked and could not agree. As the vicar, he saw the pub as the enemy, which put me in league with the very spiritual forces that the church was trying to overcome. "Well," I said, "if that's the way you feel, you must go ahead and include it in whatever you write about me to the selectors. I appreciate your telling me." I never saw what he wrote, but I couldn't help thinking that it might actually have helped my chances of being selected.

Eventually, I was asked to attend a selection conference at a convent in Chester. There were about twenty of us candidates from all over the country. We were to be watched, interviewed, and assessed over the weekend, and I was nervous about being scrutinized so closely.

There were certain tasks assigned to us to enable the selectors to observe our suitability for ministry in the church. One such task was that each of us had to lead a discussion. We had to introduce the topic, open up and chair the short discussion, then, at the end, sum up what had been said. The selectors watched to see how well we listened to what people said, how good we were at drawing quieter people into the discussion, and so on.

Part of the weekend was spent writing a pastoral letter. Each of us was given a fictitious person in a crisis to write to. I had to write to someone in my parish who had just been sent to prison. There were other practical exercises and four different selectors formally interviewed us. Even mealtimes were spent talking to selectors and to one another. It was an intense time and, when the evening service was over, a small group of us decided to walk to the local pub, hoping that it wouldn't be disapproved of.

A few weeks later I received a letter from Ronald Bowlby, the bishop of Southwark. I could barely bring myself to open it. "The course of my life depends on the contents of this letter," I thought to myself and then quickly ripped it open. It read:

Dear Joy,

I am happy to be able to tell you that, as a result of the selection conference which you recently attended, the Bishop's selectors recommended you for training as a Deaconess. I am pleased to endorse their recommendation. The selectors gained the impression that you are growing in confidence and maturity. They comment particularly on your open and enquiring mind and that you have thought clearly about current theological issues. They noted that you were able to relate well to other people. . . .

With prayers and best wishes,

Yours sincerely,

Bishop Ronald

I was so happy — it was like opening an exam results letter and discovering that I had passed. As the euphoria wore off, reality began to take hold and I began to worry. Just exactly how big was this sacrifice going to be? I might never have a boyfriend again — after all, who would want to be a vicar's husband?

I would have to go to theological college. Would it be like joining a convent or monastery? Would everyone be terribly serious and holy? Would life, as I knew it, come to an end? It was a leap of faith into the unknown and I was nervous. Eventually, I stopped worrying and remembered my promise to God and myself that I could, should, and would be myself.

On what felt like my last summer of freedom before going to theological college, I went with my friends to a Bruce Springsteen concert at Wembley Stadium. I danced my heart out as I imagined I might never do again. I shaved my hair up the sides and dyed the spiky top blonde, leaving long dark hair at the back. It was my last chance to be wild before I entered the respectable world of the Church of England — starting with the "vicar factory."

One of my selectors at the conference had recommended Cranmer Hall, Durham, for theological college. I already had an interview lined up at Trinity College, Bristol. My dad had trained there when it was Tyndale Hall: I had to make a choice. George Carey (now the archbishop of Canterbury) was the principal at Trinity when I applied, and he interviewed me. I liked him and liked the college, but they were unable to offer me a place until the following year. Now that I had been accepted for training, I really wanted to begin as soon as possible, so I decided to take a serious look at Cranmer Hall in Durham. Of course, it didn't make an ounce of difference that Cranmer Hall is the only theological college in the country with a bar!

Chapter Five

The Making of a
Modern Woman Priest

The high-speed train from Paddington Station to Durham began to slow down. As it rumbled closer to its destination, I watched eagerly out the window for my first view of this historic city. I wasn't disappointed. The light of the sky was just right, and the dark silhouettes of the cathedral and castle were quite stunning.

Durham station is high on a hill and, as I walked out with my map in hand, I was confronted again with the amazing sight of the cathedral and castle surrounded by cobbled streets, ancient houses, colleges, and churches, all neatly wrapped by the River Wear and its famous bridges. I felt a mixture of excitement and fear. The place felt so good, but what would the college be like? My interview at Cranmer Hall was to take place over the next two days, and I had no idea what to expect. Cranmer Hall was a part of St. John's College at Durham University and I found it perfectly situated on The Bailey — the cobbled street that led from the small city center up past the cathedral grounds and onto the bridge crossing the river.

The "Guest Master," a student called Steve who had the job of welcoming people, met me. "Welcome to Cranmer," he said. "Let's put your bags in the guest room and you can meet some students before your first interview." Steve led me through a rabbit warren of corridors, up and down staircases, until we came to a tiny staircase that led to the very top of the building. On either side of the staircase was a student bedroom. Steve threw open the door and ushered me in. I couldn't believe my eyes. In a room filled with cigar smoke were six students. Four of them were playing cards and the other two were eating cheese and drinking wine. The music of Sade played softly in the background. "Hey, everyone, this is Joy," said Steve. "She's here for an interview."

"Well," said one of the guys, "this is the most important question you'll be asked today: do you play bridge?"

"Actually, I do," I said, feeling a mixture of surprise and relief that these were theological college students doing some of the things I really enjoyed. I was beginning to feel much more enthusiastic about the whole experience. I made up the second four and began what would turn out to be the first of many games of bridge played within those hallowed walls. There was hardly any choice to make between colleges. I so enjoyed my interview experience and the people I met in Durham that I immediately decided that it was the place for me.

I trained three years for ministry in the Church of England. When I started in the autumn of 1985, I was one of five other women in my year who would have exactly the same training as our fifty male colleagues. We were to be licensed as deaconesses, which was an order of lay ministry, while the men would be ordained deacons for

one year and then ordained priests. It was clearly an odd
situation.

One afternoon in 1987, a group of us were listening
to the proceedings of the House of Commons on BBC
radio. We were jubilant as we listened to them approve
the Synod's decision to allow women to be ordained into
the holy order of deacon. This meant that, when we completed our training, we would become clergy alongside
the men. We would be able to wear clerical collars and be
referred to as "The Reverend."

This was a milestone of great magnitude toward priesthood for women. Most people would see a woman deacon
in service and ask the question, "Okay, if you're a deacon, what's the difference between you and a priest? You
all look the same to me. . . . " It was a good question. The
difference, I learned, is threefold. Only a priest can say
the prayer of thanksgiving over the bread and wine; only
a priest can pray the prayer of absolution, that is, declare
God's forgiveness after the confession of sins; and only a
priest can bless a group of people. In my six years as a
deacon, it was a question I answered hundreds of times.

My first year at Cranmer Hall was an adventure. I
quickly became great friends with Susie, who was about
my age. We looked a little alike and people would sometimes get us mixed up. Susie's room was next door to
mine and our windows overlooked the beautiful yard
complete with croquet lawn. Alvin, from New York City,
was across the way, Nigel was next to him, then Pete, and
Rod was a little further around the corner. Rod had been
a teacher in Africa. He was a fine chap to have as a neighbor, especially as he invited us in most evenings for a gin
and tonic before dinner.

There was plenty of classroom study at theological college, including liturgy, systematic theology, Old and New Testament studies, church history, ethics, pastoral studies, and missiology, which stretched and broadened my mind. We had excellent teachers. When classes were over, students would often debate and argue late into the night about one theological issue or another.

What made our conversations even more enlightening and enriching was the wide range of backgrounds that Cranmer students came from. It can often be the case that a theological college gets labeled as evangelical, Anglo-Catholic, or middle-of-the-road liberal. Some colleges were known to welcome gay students and some were good for women. Each had its own identity and churchmanship. Cranmer Hall had been described to me as having evangelical roots, but being very open. I trained alongside every type of Anglican and believe it helped to prevent any of us from becoming too entrenched in a particular tradition.

Soon after the first term began, Susie and I set off on a shopping trip to Newcastle: we needed to get fitted up for our clerical clothes. We had each been assigned to an area of on-the-job training called "pastoral placements" and would need at least some of our gear before ordination. A cassock and surplice were basic requirements. We had asked a friend in the year above us where we should go. "The place you need to find is called J & M's in Newcastle. It's a small business run by two women who make all the vestments themselves."

The train took twenty minutes to reach Newcastle. We found what we thought was the right street and number, and we stood outside. It didn't look like a clerical outfitter, more like someone's house.

"Well, they did say it was just a small business. Maybe they work from home," I ventured. So we rang the bell and a little old lady came to the door.

"Hello. Is this J & M's?" asked Susie.

"Why aye!" replied the woman in a strong Geordie accent. "Jack and Molly, come on in."

We looked at each other. "Jack and Molly!" Susie whispered. "Uhm, do you make cassocks?" I asked.

"Well, I have tried my hand at a little embroidery. What is a cassock exactly? One of them things you rest your feet on?" Molly asked.

We gently explained that a cassock was a black robe worn by clergy and that we had knocked on her door by mistake. Molly was thrilled that we visited her and it turned out to be good pastoral training. We made our way to the real J & M's giggling like teenagers. A week later Susie acquired two goldfish and we named them Jack and Molly.

For our pastoral placements, Susie was assigned to a local church and I was assigned to the hospital visiting team. Every Sunday afternoon the hospital team was let loose on the wards of the local infirmary. I visited women on the gynecological ward for an hour or so and then wheeled any patients who wanted to attend down to the chapel for a church service. It was our responsibility as a team to lead the singing, the prayers, and the Bible readings and to preach the sermon. When it was finished, we wheeled the patients back to their wards.

One Sunday I spent most of the afternoon with a woman who'd had a hysterectomy. She began to open her heart to me. She tearfully told me that her husband had died the year before. "We were on vacation when he began to have chest pains. I didn't know what to do. We decided to get on the train and head back home where his doctor was. On the way home, he died on the train. I've been guilt-ridden ever since."

It was the first time I had been in this position. I was expected to respond as a chaplain, give words of comfort and assurance. I prayed what I call an "arrow prayer," a prayer shot straight up, without frills, which I often use when in a tight spot. "Please God, give me the words for this poor woman." I held her hand and assured her that God understood and didn't blame her and that she shouldn't blame herself. I tried to give other words of spiritual comfort. Then all of a sudden I said something that was not especially helpful. "Well, at least he was with someone he loved when he died." She just nodded and sniffed. I know now that the most important things I did that day were to listen and hold her hand. My words were inconsequential.

Susie and I talked and laughed about the many unhelpful and insensitive things that we found ourselves saying in an effort to be caring. We compiled a mental notebook of "Useful Pastoral Phrases" that kept us chuckling for a long time. It contained sayings like, "Never mind eh?" "It could be worse," and "There's plenty more fish in the sea."

For one week every year, six Cranmer students were given the opportunity to exchange with six students from the Roman Catholic seminary in Durham. I had become friends with an American girl who was studying with us for one year on a Rotary scholarship. Cheri was from Texas and was training to be a Methodist minister in the United States. We both thought the exchange would be a wonderful experience and signed up.

Ushaw Seminary was big and old and full of young men training to be Catholic priests. Most of them had come straight from school and 80 percent would drop out before the final commitment of ordination. The training itself was part of the selection procedure, so there was a real mixed bag of lads. In the Anglican system, we went through selection before going to college. Unless anything really ugly happened, all of us in our year would get to ordination.

The Catholic lads were mostly down-to-earth, working-class Northerners. I liked them a lot and often felt more at home with friends I made at Ushaw than with those from my own college. The large common room at Ushaw had an unusual feature: a well-stocked bar that stretched across the entire top end of the room. It was open on Wednesday and Sunday evenings and had an enormous crucifix hanging on the wall above. As the week progressed our friendships deepened and our understanding of each other's spirituality broadened.

During the exchange week we joined in the daily offices of the Catholic Church, that is, we went to all the services — Morning Prayer, Evening Prayer, and Mass — every day. The most difficult thing for us Cranmer students was to experience the reality that we could not receive the bread and wine in the Catholic Mass. We were living in community with our Catholic brothers: we ate together, drank together, prayed together, and played together, but, when it came to sharing in the ultimate expression of our holy communion, we were excluded by the rulings of the Catholic Church. It was painful for all of us, but I had decided at the very beginning that it should not be any more divisive than it had to be. I have often said that I love the church, but believe in a

God who is not bound by it. I participated fully in the service and, when it came time to receive, I went to the priest in line with everyone else. When faced with me, a non-Catholic, the priest — usually a good friend — gave me a blessing. On my part, I received the bread and wine "spiritually," internally ignoring the rulings of the powers that be and thanking God for the spiritual nourishment of the community.

AT THE START of our second year at Cranmer, Susie and I moved out of college accommodation and found what we considered to be the very best place to live in the whole of Durham. Canon Professor Dan Hardy and his wife, Perrin, had just arrived in town. Their wonderful home was located in the Cathedral Close, at Number 14, The College. All their children had grown and they wanted to let the top floor of their house to students. Professor Hardy just happened to mention this while having dinner with us one evening in the Cranmer Hall dining room. Susie and I jumped at the chance and made an appointment to see Mrs. Hardy as soon as possible.

"Now girls, we would just love to have you live upstairs," said Perrin with her softened American accent. "I've already let the third room to a lovely girl called Katie. She's a mature student studying zoology. I'm sure you'll get along just fine." And we did. The friendships that formed between the three of us that year were the kind that last forever and the links between us are still strong.

We each had our own room with arched, stained-glass windows that looked directly onto the imposing towers of Durham Cathedral. We shared a small lounge. The large window in the lounge opened onto a flat roof and, on balmy summer nights, we would invite people over for drinks, strawberries, and ice cream. At the end of the hallway was our bathroom. Its window had the most spectacular view of the River Wear and a pink cottage on the opposite bank. It was sometimes difficult to leave.

Katie may technically have been a "mature student," but she wasn't at all what we expected. At thirty years old, she was beautiful, blonde, and a lot of fun. She was extremely sweet natured and loved animals. She had a cockatoo that lived with her in her room, and Katie called me "Joyo." One evening, Katie came home to a roomful of Cranmer students. She had been out to visit friends and was much later than we expected her to be. "Is everything okay?" asked Susie. Much to our amusement and delight she told us this story.

"I had a lovely time with my friends and left their house a long time ago. On the way home my car broke down. I could see lights from a house about three hundred yards away, but otherwise the road was deserted. So, I walked to the house, asked to use their phone to call the tow truck. The man on the other end of the phone told me to stay with the car. So, I went back and waited. They took a long time to arrive and I was desperate to go to the bathroom. I hopped around with my legs crossed for a while and then decided to squat down right there behind the car. I felt much better and soon after that the tow truck arrived. He opened the hood, had a look around, and then said knowingly, 'Ahh! Look! It's a gas leak!' 'No, no,' I said feeling rather embarrassed, 'I'm sure that's not gas.' Then the mechanic got down on his knees, dipped his finger in the liquid, licked it, and said, 'Yes, ma'am, that's gas all right.'"

I continued to visit my friends at the Ushaw Seminary and was frequently invited to dinner there on Wednesday evenings, when the college was open to visitors. One time I was propping up the bar with Sister Cecily, the only woman on the staff. Both of us were drinking pints of beer. Peter Wright, one of the students, approached me. "Joy, we are putting on a play at the end of next term. It's a play about St. Francis of Assisi called *Poor Fool,* and we were wondering if you would play the part of St. Clare." Peter was to direct the play, which was written by Richard Cooper, and obviously there was a real shortage of possible Clares around the place — that is, if Clare was to be played by a woman! I loved the idea and said yes almost immediately.

Weeks of rehearsals followed, and I spent a lot of time at Ushaw with new friends. I especially liked Paul, who played Francis in the production. I will never forget the day of our first rehearsal. Peter wanted us all to get to know each other. "Get into twos, Francis with Clare, and others find partners. Simply talk to each other for ten minutes and find out about each other's lives." I needed a bathroom break and excused myself. While I was gone, Paul pleaded with Peter to give him a different partner. "Peter, I can't do this. I can't talk to a woman for ten minutes. I've never really talked to a woman before. Please don't make me do it!" Paul was barely nineteen years old and had been sheltered in a Catholic secondary school designed to prepare boys for the seminary. He really was scared of women! On my return, the "getting to know you" exercise began and it was the start of a firm friendship that lasts until this day.

Another friend in the play, Edmond, took me to visit the Claretian sisters at their convent. Edmond had called the sisters and told them about the play, and they were willing to lend me a habit to wear as my costume. We had a wonderful visit. The sisters showed me how to put on the wimple and habit. Over tea and cakes, we talked to one another about our respective callings. They were great women, and I know they prayed for me regularly for years after.

So there I was as St. Clare, wearing the genuine clothing, performing for three consecutive nights and a matinee. It was my first serious foray into acting and I loved it. In a press release, the producer Mark said, "It seems fitting that the roles of St. Francis and St. Clare should bring together our two churches in paying tribute to this great saint of peace and brotherly love." I discovered a real love for St. Francis (the saint, not the actor!) and, when I spoke my final lines as Francis lay dying, I wept real tears at every performance. Francis says, "If only He hadn't picked a fool for His laborer," and the final lines are Clare's response:

"I was praying last night, and I saw something so clearly. I saw a road. And on that road all the great saints of the church were walking. Popes, bishops, with the gold of their robes all shining in the morning sun. And a crowd, a huge, huge crowd of ordinary folk. And, as they walked, all of them had their eyes on the ground, finding the footprints of Christ and fearful lest they lost them.

"Then, at the very end of the procession, there was a little man, not handsome and his clothes in rags. And *his* head was back as he sang a great song to the glory of God, His world, and His making. He didn't look down. He never took his eyes off heaven. Poor fool. Poor, poor fool."

Never before St. Francis's life had I encountered one so consumed with the Gospel, a man so on fire with the love of God, a disciple so focused on following Jesus, a spirit so joyful in abandoning everything to serve his Lord. I saw Christ incarnate in the life of St. Francis and it was like meeting Jesus afresh. Francis seemed to be converting me all over again. I cried each night, partly because my faith seemed so small and weak in comparison.

Before beginning my third and final year at theological college, I spent the summer on placement in the United States. Mike Williams, my personal tutor, had managed to put me in touch with the Lutheran seminary in Chicago, and I had also made a contact in the Episcopal Church in Virginia. "Joy, it will be good to compare and contrast the two experiences. The north and south of America are very different places. We'll need a full report when you come back," said Mike.

My host in Chicago, Hope Davies, met me at the airport with a small group of teenagers. Four of them were her own kids — Jennifer, Theresa, Michael, and Donald — and one was their friend, Larry. It was quite a welcome, with just about enough room in the van for me and my bag. "The accommodation that was lined up for you has fallen through, so you'll be staying with us tonight and we'll sort something out tomorrow," announced Hope. We drove into the South Side of Chicago and pulled in behind their apartment building. "I'm training to be a Lutheran minister," said Hope, "and this is where we're living for a few years. It's quite close to the seminary." The apartment was very small, especially for a family of five, and my presence was going to make it a very tight squeeze. Theresa already slept on the couch in the living room.

The next day the kids gathered round and informed me that they liked having me around and, if it was okay with me, they'd like me to stay with them for the whole three weeks. It proved to be a good decision. Hope was a mature student with a lot of life experience. She had amazing energy and passion for the two small, black congregations she was serving, and I was immersed into that energy immediately as I accompanied and assisted her.

Most evenings, at the end of the day, we would sit on her balcony and she would tell me story after story that helped me to understand African American culture and history. Most of her essays for the seminary were written on, or related to, that topic, and I devoured them. I attended meetings and Bible studies of local clergy who were mainly black, and I was fascinated by the way they did business. There was energy and vibrancy as they foraged after the truth of the Scriptures. It was not unusual or unacceptable for fist banging and yelling to be a part of the exchange of ideas. "I hear you brother, I hear you!" would often be shouted out after a point had been forcefully made. It was so much more exciting than the more polite Bible studies I was used to.

One Sunday I was invited to preach and very soon learned that I needed to leave some spaces for the shouts of "Amen," "Well?" and "Preach it, sister." It really lifted my whole preaching style that day. "I love these congregations!" I thought to myself, and made a mental note that a black neighborhood or at least a diverse congregation was going to be important to me when I looked for my first job.

The tiny country church in Virginia was indeed a very different experience. The church itself looked like as if it had been lifted straight from the top of a wedding cake.

The church was very white, and I soon learned that this was true of the congregation as well. What I encountered there in the Deep South was a shock to my system, especially after the wonderful time I had just had with the black churches in Chicago.

Adult Sunday school classes are a strong tradition in American churches, and they usually happen in the morning before the main service begins. I was teaching the class for three weeks on the book of Genesis. We had worked our way through the interesting creation stories and, that week, I was taking some questions after working through the story of Cain and Abel. After Cain killed Abel, God banished him and marked him with the "mark of Cain." It was actually God's promise that, even though he had been banished, he would not be harmed. An elderly gentleman raised his hand and said in a Southern drawl, "Excuse me, ma'am, but I've always been taught that the 'mark of Cain' was that God made him black."

The legacy of slavery and segregation in the South was still strong. It was rooted in the way people understood their world and in the way they interpreted their Bible. No one would openly say they were racist, but I found racism not too far beneath the surface.

The woman who played the organ in that Virginia church had recently handed in her notice, and they were advertising for a replacement. I was at the vestry meeting (parish council) where they were to look at the applications. Sadly, there had not been a great response, but there was one applicant who was fabulously qualified. He had music qualifications and lots of good experience. He was a committed Christian, and I could see no one better. The "problem," it turned out, was that he was black. After some awkward discussion, someone finally spluttered, "I just don't think this church is ready for a black person yet." I was bursting to say something but, as an observer, could not. After the meeting, I was livid with anger.

"How can they do this?" I asked the rector. "Don't they understand that they have just violated the basic principles of Christianity?"

"Joy, the most powerful man in the church is putting pressure on the members of the vestry to vote the way he wants," replied the rector.

"But what makes him so powerful?" I asked. "Why can't people ignore him and do the right thing?"

Even though one of the wealthiest men in the church was against the idea, the vestry, to their credit, did eventually offer the job to the black organist. By that time, however, he had found another position. I certainly had experienced very different churches and very different cultures. It was an education.

I FLEW HOME to England eager to begin my third and final year of training. I was especially excited because I was to move in to Ushaw Seminary for the first term of the year. It was the first time in Ushaw's history that they had an honorary woman seminarian. Surprisingly, I was accepted without too much fuss by both the staff and students. I had slowly got to know folks at the seminary in the previous two years, and for me to move there in the final year wasn't too much of a shock. Some people were a little uncomfortable that a young woman was to be living amid young men preparing to take vows of celibacy. The monsignor, however, commented, "I'm just happy to know that some of the boys have red blood in their veins!"

I so valued my exposure to Catholic spirituality. It was different enough from my own to be new and exciting,

With friends at Ushaw
Roman Catholic
Seminary in Durham,
1985.

yet felt comfortable and rooted in the real world. One morning I was sitting in the enormous chapel for Morning Prayer. The great, carved wooden choir stalls swallowed us up, and I would often sit there meditating, wearing slippers on my feet. I suddenly realized that it was my group's turn this week to give the readings and lead the services and that I had been assigned to read the Scripture that morning. Father Cunningham nodded at me to move forward to the large golden eagle lectern raised up on a platform in the center of the nave. I looked down at my big pink furry slippers and panicked. "What shall I do? I can either kick them off and walk up there in bare feet or be brazen and wear the slippers. Either way, people are going to think I'm strange." In the end, I opted for the slippers and read so very dramatically that I hoped people wouldn't notice my feet.

By the time I finished at Ushaw, I had gained a great number of good friends. These men, many of whom are now priests in the Catholic Church, gave me a lot of support in the struggle toward the ordination of women. Even though the Catholic Church does not ordain women, the reality is that, at the grassroots level, many priests and, of course, women in Catholic congregations wish that it did.

When it later became clear that the Church of England would ordain women to the priesthood, it made me smile when Anglo-Catholics wanted to "go to Rome" and become Roman Catholics. The Anglo-Catholic wing of the church can sometimes be so extremely "Catholic" that they find themselves trapped in a kind of fantasyland. They no longer feel at home in a changing Church of England, and then they find that, lo and behold, the Catholic Church on the ground has also reformed and progressed. They don't feel at home there either.

AT THE END of our three years in Durham, Susie married Rod and they were ordained together to serve jointly as curates in Luton. I think it was the promise of gin and tonics forever that clinched it. The wedding was a beautiful and very clerical affair. I was one of Susie's bridesmaids. At the reception, Susie's fifteen-year-old atheist, Marxist brother, Henry, got drunk enough and brave enough to take on the abundance of clergy. As we sat in the conservatory sipping champagne, Henry burst through the doors and said something like "God is a load of crap. So which one of you vicars wants to fight me over it?" He stood there, fists held in front of his face, ready to box. As quick as a flash, Reverend Mike smiled and said, "I'm so sorry, old boy, but we're all on our day off." I'm not sure that poor Henry has ever been allowed to forget that incident. Susie went on to have two girls, Abigail and Rebecca. Katie went on to have a little boy, Jamie; and I am a proud godmother to Abi and Jamie.

I was grateful for my three years' training in Durham. It felt a bit like a hothouse experience: I was removed from the day-to-day reality of life in South London but given intense exposure to new ways of understanding God and people from different backgrounds. I moved through a sharp learning curve, theologically, spiritually, and personally. I had one or two romantic entanglements and fell in and out of love with a fellow ordinand — several times! I finally settled down to the fact that, at least for now, I was called to do this ministry thing as a single person.

Ordination to the deaconate loomed. I was thankful to have a job to go to, because the laws of the Church of England state that, if you don't have a church to go to, you cannot be ordained. The meaning of the Greek word for deacon is "one who serves." So it makes sense that no one should become a deacon with no group of people or community to serve after the ordination service. The church and community I was about to serve was the Parish of St. James, Hatcham, in New Cross. More specifically, I was to be the minister of the daughter church, St. Michael's, on the Milton Court Estate, otherwise known as "Crack City."

Chapter Six

New Cross

I was hired as the minister in charge of St. Michael's Church and the warden of the community center. Did I get the job because I was absolutely the right person they had been looking for, or were they so desperate that they would take anyone willing to go? The post had been vacant for two years.

Applicants had come and gone, turning the job down for one reason or another. Men with families were unprepared to live in such a potentially dangerous environment. I'll never know for sure what influenced the selectors' decision, but there I was, fresh from college, a single woman, still wet behind the ears, not allowed to be a priest and taking a job that scared the hell out of most men.

In all fairness, it was a tough placement and bore no resemblance to the rural idyll found in the parish of Dibley. St. Michael's was a small congregation with around twenty-five core members in attendance each Sunday. About half of them lived on the Milton Court Estate, and the other half lived in the wider parish of St. James, Hatcham. The estate in Deptford, southeast London, was nestled in between New Cross and New Cross Gate train stations. The ugly, high-rise tower blocks of Milton Court Estate dwarfed rows of identical flats. A halfhearted attempt to relieve this dismal scene with green patches had resulted in mini-wastelands amid the gray concrete.

The church and community center had been built in the 1960s and had a lot of potential. A third of the building housed a nursery for children at risk and a play group. This area was well equipped with a kitchen, toilets, and an office. In another third there was a big gymnasium with marked courts and basketball nets. The church sanctuary and community meeting rooms accounted for the remaining third. Above this great space were three flats. Two of them were on the second floor above the community center. The third, on the top floor, was the warden's flat — my new home. It stretched all the way across the building and had a roof garden. It was bright, spacious, and even had a large office/meeting room with a separate entrance from the stairwell. Inside, there was a door connecting the meeting room to the rest of the flat. "If I can make this flat my safe haven, my sanctuary, I know I can face the difficulties that may arise," I thought to myself.

The best thing about this new home was that I had someone to share it with. Ruth was to be my flatmate for the next four years. She had been a student at Newcastle University while I was in Durham. Her boyfriend, Mark, had been at Cranmer with me, training to be a priest, and Ruth and I had got to know each other on her frequent visits. Mark was now the new curate at Christ Church, Purley, where my dad was the vicar. It was all very cozy, and all of us traveled back and forth between New Cross and Purley on a regular basis.

Ruth divided her weekends, spending every other Sunday in Purley. She had to make sure all the young women in the Christ Church congregation knew that the hand-some new curate was spoken for! Ruth was a newly qualified teacher and had found a job in the East End of London. She was a bundle of energy and fun. Everyone loved her, and she was a great support at St. Michael's. It wasn't unusual to find Ruth comforting an elderly lady after church or listening sympathetically to someone who was mentally ill. Ruth would often use her gift of dance in the service to enhance the worship, or would step in to play the piano when David, our very talented teenage organist, wasn't available.

Later, when writer Richard Curtis created the character of Alice for the TV show *The Vicar of Dibley,* he had no idea that Ruth existed. Alice had an uncanny physical resemblance to Ruth and was a close friend of Geraldine, the TV vicar. Much like Alice in *The Vicar of Dibley,* Ruth was enthusiastically available to support me in many ways, but, unlike Alice, she was totally competent at just about everything!

Living and working in South London meant that I was able to be close to my brother, Ray, and his family. Ray has always been one of my best friends; he is one of the most fun people I know and I feel very fortunate to be his sister. Ray is the kind of bloke everyone wants to have at their party or social event. He has a quick wit and a kind heart.

In 1986, when he was twenty-three, Ray got married to Julie, who lived in Liverpool. Julie had a five-year-old son, Jacob, and so Ray became an instant dad with a ready-made family. In 1988, Ben was born and, four years later, Stephen. These beautiful, wonderful boys were very special to me, and I loved living close enough to share in their growing up. They often came to stay at my house,

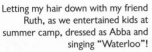

Letting my hair down with my friend
Ruth, as we entertained kids at
summer camp, dressed as Abba and
singing "Waterloo"!

and we enjoyed lots of outings and trips together. Ray and his family kept me sane and with them I felt rooted and at home. Most of all, I enjoyed being able to spend an afternoon or an evening just hanging out at their home in West Norwood, sharing in their everyday lives.

Ray loves to tease and play practical jokes on people and, one night, he well and truly "got me." I had just moved to New Cross and needed a filling in one of my teeth. Guy's Hospital, at London Bridge, is a university hospital that also trains dentists, and my colleagues recommended I go there. I was wearing my clerical collar as I had come straight from a meeting at the cathedral. My dentist was a handsome young man who told me, during the one-way type of conversation one has with a dentist, that he was a pianist at another church in London. The dentist later phoned me, and we went out for a meal together. I thought I might see him again, but Ruth was adamant that I shouldn't go to his place until he had been "checked out" by her. "He could be a mad axe man, Joy. You don't know him at all!" He'd seemed pretty safe to me.

On Ruth's advice, I invited the dentist to come over to our flat for dinner to meet her. I also invited Ray and

Julie — and that was my big mistake! I was keen to make
a good impression and wanted the dentist to feel at home
with everyone. He arrived first and seemed a little nervous. Ruth chatted with him over a glass of wine while
I finished cooking in the kitchen. Soon, everything was
ready and the doorbell rang: Ray and Julie had arrived.
I dashed eagerly to the door and swung it open. There
stood Ray and Julie dressed up to look like twits. Ray
had flared, tartan trousers on, which were too short for
him, a very tight T-shirt, and a kerchief knotted on his
head. In his hand he held a bottle of wine wrapped up
in newspaper. "Ello," he said in a thick, heavy voice, "I
brought you a bottle of me 'ome made."

Julie followed, wearing a bright red, Crimplene trouser
suit with her hair tied up in pigtails. Her bright red lipstick was smeared on her teeth. I was completely taken by
surprise as Ray bounded past me and extended his wrong
hand to the dentist to shake, with a "Pleased to meet ya."

Ray and Julie kept up the act long enough to have the
dentist wondering who on earth he had got involved with.
I wasn't sure whether to laugh or cry. Ruth was doing both
in the kitchen as she clutched her stomach: she had been
in on the prank with Ray from the beginning. The dentist
never really relaxed that evening and didn't hang around
too long. Poor fellow.

As a clergy person in New Cross, I belonged to the
Deptford Chapter of clergy. A friend of mine always
laughed as he imagined me going to meet with a chapter
of bikers — Hell's Angels perhaps. Clergy from the Deptford area would gather on a regular basis to discuss issues
and deal with any church or local business. The first time
I walked into that meeting, I heard one new colleague say

to his neighbor, "What is that?" He was referring to me, a woman wearing a clerical collar. He was opposed to the ordination of women and clearly did not like what he saw.

That was the first and last time that I experienced hostility from my colleagues in Deptford. We all became firm friends and were supportive of one another in ministry. Father Owen was one of those who did not want to see women ordained. He was the chaplain of the Millwall Football Club and a wonderful priest to the whole community in New Cross Gate. After I preached at his church one Sunday, he complimented me on my ability to communicate the gospel. Also, there was Father David Diamond, a well-known and much loved Anglo-Catholic priest at St. Paul's, Deptford. He, too, was opposed to the ordination of women, but we became great friends. I joined in helping with his church's ministry to the homeless in the crypt of St. Paul's. He also welcomed me to his pulpit many times.

When Father Diamond died, after more than twenty-five years of exceptional priestly care in Deptford, his funeral was an extravagant affair. I sat in the congregation because I was unable to be a part of the massive clergy procession. Father Diamond would have wanted me to process, but too many of his friends would have found it upsetting. Many clergy softened and some even changed their minds about the ordination of women when they rubbed shoulders with real women colleagues who were doing a good job in the communities they loved. I will never forget the moment at the funeral when a homeless man staggered up to the coffin, slapped his hand on it, and said in a drunken slur, "You were all right, you old bastard."

In 1986, while I was at theological college, the Church of England had produced a report called "Faith in the City." It was an analysis of the problems in the nation's inner cities and contained recommendations as to how the problems could be overcome by both church and government. The report was condemned by many in the Conservative Party as a Marxist document written by a church that should keep itself out of politics and concentrate on the care of people's souls.

Almost overnight, the report put an end to the church's image as "the Tory Party at prayer": concern for the poor was no longer the domain of the lefty clerical fringe and one or two radical bishops. With "Faith in the City," the whole church had put its weight behind our Christian duty to take a more active role in addressing the mounting social problems caused by the decline of the inner cities, whatever the political implications.

"Faith in the City" was an extremely significant document for me as I was to be working in one of the neighborhoods that the report called "Urban Priority Areas." The report set the agenda in many ways for the next ten years and the Church Urban Fund was set up to enable the hoped-for regeneration to take place in churches and communities across the land.

We were all expected to support the Church Urban Fund in any way we could. Even small churches that would possibly end up benefiting from the fund had to raise a small amount. It was the Church Urban Fund that called me one day and asked if I would take part in a sponsored rappel down the side of a very tall church tower: St. Lawrence Jewry in the City of London.

The *Church of England Newspaper* reported it as follows, under the headline: "Jumping for Joy."

My terrifying sponsored rappel, down the tower of St. Lawrence, Jewry, for the Church Urban Fund.

"The look of terror on her face says it all. Lurching out backwards over a parapet 150 feet above the street below is never a comfortable exercise — even if you are a fully trained Marine. But when you are the Rev. Joy Carroll, a female curate in South London, rappelling isn't exactly your average day's work.

"However, this leap of faith paid great dividends. Grasping the rope firmly and following the instructions of the soldier above, London's most glamorous priest made a safe descent from St. Lawrence Jewry to the pavement below, and collected more than £400 for charity in the process."

The rappel was terrifying as I went over the edge. I had done a parachute jump the year before and thought this would be a piece of cake in comparison. But when I had one leg over the parapet, there wasn't a single part of my body that wanted to follow it. Then I remembered that I actually had to be pushed out of the plane. Doing a parachute jump, that moment of commitment to the task, was taken care of for me by someone else. Going over the edge of the church tower was something I had to do all by myself. I did finally manage to let go of the nice soldier.

I was in very mixed company at that charity event. Merchant bankers, solicitors, and insurance brokers from the City rubbed shoulders with church commissioners and staff from the Church Urban Fund. Even the television impersonator Rory Bremner joined in the fun. In fact, he enjoyed it so much he went back up to do it again — three times. The people who took part that day managed to raise over £10,000 for the fund.

St. Michael's was my starting ground for neighborhood regeneration. The ugliness of Milton Court was not the worst of its problems. The area had long been notorious for its organized drug trade. A few months after I arrived, a police raid unearthed a home factory manufacturing the highly addictive cocaine-based drug "crack." The estate was already being referred to as "Crack City." Most children did not play in the uncared-for playgrounds on the estate, and most adults would not drink in the pub: it was drug-dealer territory.

Lucky for me, Kim Hitch and Barry Carter were both veteran inner-city ministers. Because St. Michael's was an ecumenical church — both Anglican and United Reformed — I had both Kim and Barry as my bosses. Kim was responsible for my training on the job. He was to help form my spiritual and occupational disciplines in those

early years, and I was accountable to him and my bishops for day-to-day ministry. These were indeed days of
training and, in my enthusiasm, I made a goodly number
of mistakes. Barry and Kim, with all their combined experience, looked on. They were always on hand to support
or help pick up the pieces. They must have felt like parents often feel as they watch their children make mistakes,
learning their first hard lessons in life.

One of my mistakes happened almost immediately. At
college, we had been encouraged to develop a good and
positive relationship with the local press. "If you scratch
their back, they'll scratch yours," we were told. In return
for cooperating with interesting local news or human-
interest stories, they would be much more predisposed
to highlight or even cover church events. So when the
Deptford Mercury ran an article about the new woman
curate on the Milton Court Estate, I was quite pleased
with the result. The headline was: "Reverend Joy: New
Guardian for SE London Housing Estate." The reporter,
Pat Greenwood, was a kindly, middle-aged woman, and
she did a good job of introducing this newly ordained
twenty-nine-year-old to the community.

The next day, the entry phone to the church building
buzzed. I picked up the receiver. "Hello there, my name is
Graham," said a friendly voice, "and I'm an independent
writer for the *Daily Express*. I've just read about you in
the *Mercury* and wondered if I could interview you about
your new job and the drug problems on the estate."

"Well," I replied cautiously, "I can't tell you anything
about the drug situation because I really don't know anything substantial, but I can tell you about some of the
wonderful projects going on here and some of my hopes
for the future — you know, good stuff."

"Okay," he replied, "that sounds great." I hopped down the three flights of stairs, let him into the building, and we walked through to the office. I spent a long time telling him about the nursery for children at risk and the little church that met here every Sunday morning. I shared some of my hopes of getting the building into shape and using it even more extensively for the community. He scribbled as I wrote and seemed very interested. Just as he left and I stood at the door to see him off, a photographer jumped out of his parked car. "You don't mind if he takes a couple of shots do you?" I felt like I didn't have much choice.

The next day, January 19, 1989, the article appeared in the *Daily Express,* and I was mortified. "Crusader of Crack City — Curate Joy fights to make estate safe as danger drug threatens children," read the headlines on page five.

The article began, "Crusading Joy Carroll stands in the front line against an evil drug epidemic which police fear is about to swamp Britain. Trendy, raven-haired Joy, 29, is the curate of a church in the middle of an estate known to locals as 'Crack City.' "

Not only was I misquoted, but the reporter completely fabricated whole statements, such as, "I've got to protect the kids from drugs. This place must not be turned into a hell hole." He made it sound as if it was just little me standing between the drug barons and the police: "Her caring crusade against the drug peddlers and criminal racketeers who live on the estate is supported by the six police constables who walk the infamous Beat 17."

I couldn't believe how much this reporter had misrepresented, distorted, and largely ignored what I had actually said. I'd had my fingers burned and suddenly felt very vulnerable. I had nightmares about having bricks thrown through my window with notes attached: "It's time for you to leave"! The last thing I wanted or needed was for local people to think I was there to clean up their estate, when what I wanted most of all was to win their trust and earn their respect. "How am I going to fix this?" I wailed to Barry as I showed him the *Express* article. "I think I can help," he smiled.

The Spanish Steps on the Milton Court Estate was not what one would describe as a family pub. It was a very shady place, which most people either avoided or wandered into by mistake. I was nervous as I walked through the doors and approached the bar with Barry. I was wearing my clerical collar. It was on such occasions as this that it felt like a suit of armor. Most people in the black community were either stunned to see it on a woman or full of respect for it. "Thank God for the spirituality of their grandmothers," I would often think.

"I'll have half a lager, thanks Barry," I said. We moved around the corner of the bar with our drinks where a small group of hefty-looking young men were gathered. The gold of their chains and watches glistened in the gloom of the pub.

"Headley," said Barry, "I want you to meet a friend of mine, the Reverend Joy Carroll. She's working with me on the estate. In fact, she baptized your cousin's baby two weeks ago." Headley shook my hand, "Pleased to meet you. What can I do for you?" Headley was well-respected by a great number of people in the community, including the gangs and those involved in the drug trade. "Well," I ventured, "I think I may be in a spot of trouble." I explained to him what had happened and that I was concerned that people might have the wrong idea about my presence on the estate. We talked and after a while he put his big arm around my shoulder and said in a big, deep voice, "Don't you worry, darlin'. If anyone around 'ere gives you any trouble, just tell 'em you know Headley." "Headley, Headley, Headley," I repeated to myself as I walked home. I wanted to be sure to remember that name!

Kim Hitch trained me in all aspects of ministry and, for a while at the very beginning, I shadowed him on the job. "Watch and learn" was the general idea, so when the first funeral came through, I was to go along with him and see how it should be done.

"Now the first thing to remember," said Kim, "is not to be late. If you leave home just a little too late, you could find yourself stuck behind the funeral cars on the way to the cemetery and that would be a disaster. It's very bad form to arrive after the bereaved family."

We jumped into the car and Kim began to drive. Unfortunately, after giving me his words of wisdom, he had in fact left just a little too late, and who should be driving right in front of us? Yes, it was our funeral party. If Kim hadn't been wearing a clerical collar at that moment, he could have been mistaken for Sterling Moss. He put his foot down hard on the accelerator and began a brave attempt to overtake the slow-moving funeral procession. He was doing well until he reached a traffic circle.

There was no opening to continue at high speed and, all of a sudden, it became horribly clear that he would have to cut in between the coffin-bearing hearse and the family's limousine. I ducked down in the passenger seat while Kim muttered under his breath. This first lesson in how to conduct a funeral was going very wrong.

Finally, we broke away and zipped quickly on to the cemetery. As Kim calmly greeted the undertakers and family, I heard the buzz of conversation, "Did you see that maniac who cut up the procession at the traffic circle. What a disgraceful thing to do." Thankfully, Kim's car was safely out of the way in the staff parking lot, and no one ever knew that the maniac was the vicar!

RIGHT NEXT TO ST. MICHAEL'S, adjacent to the gymnasium, was a parking lot. It was council property. Perhaps I should say that it was *intended* for use as a parking lot when it was first built. If, in reality, anyone was unwise enough to actually park a car there, they would be sure to find it stripped of any valuable parts in no time at all. The space had become a dumping ground for difficult-to-dispose-of items such as old beds, refrigerators, and furniture. It was a disgusting eyesore and potential health hazard. For the third time in a month, I rang the council to have the rubbish removed. It was becoming a pain.

I walked through the parking lot with my camera around my neck. One of the little boys who attended our nursery was jumping up and down on a dirty old mattress while his mum watched. An idea was forming in my head. What if we could somehow transform this space into a beautiful park? A park where kids could play safely, where families or community groups could have barbecues, a great place for all kinds of outdoor events. I took a few photos of three-year-old Kevin jumping on the mattress amid the garbage and felt a pang of sadness that he had no park to play in. An increasing number of families were being given flats in one of the high-rise tower blocks, and the lifts broke down on a regular basis. I took some more photographs. Now that I had the evidence, perhaps I could persuade the borough of Lewisham that we could do something creative here.

With the help of the borough architect, we designed a dream park — a community park on the site of that disused parking lot. It included play equipment, a lawn area, a barbecue with picnic tables and large sheds to store outdoor play equipment for the children and gardening tools. There were to be trees, bushes, and plants and most important would be the bright yellow tall metal fence that would keep out dogs and vandals. The park was to be looked after by St. Michael's but be available to all in the community to use. I submitted an application to the government's Inner Areas Program, which included every scrap of evidence I could find that this was a good idea, along with the photographs I had taken of the site. It was very exciting, and we waited with bated breath to see if it would be approved.

In the meantime, more money was being made available to regenerate London's inner cities. We were all concerned that these funding initiatives would be short-term solutions or "fix-its" instead of long-term government policies that would ensure the regeneration of all our inner-city neighborhoods. While faithfully expressing that concern wherever possible and whenever appropriate, we wanted to find a way to work together with the government to make this particular money work for those young people who needed it most around us.

Just the night before our park application, I had braced myself to confront a group of teenage boys who had been climbing up onto the roofs of the flats below. They were terrifying the residents, banging on their windows, yelling obscenities, and threatening to throw bricks through the windows. It had happened on and off for a couple of weeks. I knew who the boys were and found them one day outside the community shops. These lads had been children in the nursery at St. Michael's. Now, twelve or thirteen years later, they were bored.

"Hey, lads, do you have a minute? I know you all came to St. Michael's when you were little kids, so you know that it's a place that is trying to make a difference on the estate. Why are you giving us a hard time? Do you know you're really frightening my neighbors?" I said with a deceptive show of confidence.

"Yeah, we know, but St. Michael's is no good to us now. It's okay for little kids but there's nothing for us. We're bored and just having a laugh." We came to an agreement that they would stop hassling St. Michael's and I would keep them informed about all the new things that were about to be made possible for kids of all ages. They had some good ideas and ended up being helpful consultants.

Gradually, with support from various government agencies and the Church Urban Fund, St. Michael's began to change and develop. We were able to employ a youth coordinator and youth workers and open a much needed and very popular after-school club. During the day, we facilitated a parent/toddler group and a toy library, where parents could borrow toys for a week in the same way one would borrow a book.

Several hundred children used the after-school club every week. The center was heaving with tired and hungry children every evening. They were fed, cared for, and entertained. Table football, pool tables, group games, and quieter activity rooms kept them happy and busy. Very soon there was a homework club, music workshops, and a dance and drama club added to the available menu. On most days, at 3:30 p.m., I would drop whatever I was doing and hang out with the kids and staff who filled the building downstairs until 6:00 p.m. In the summer vacation, the same staff ran an action-packed vacation program, taking groups out to the cinema, swimming, bowling, and so on. They were busy, tiring, but immensely worthwhile days.

Permission had come through for the community park, and the day came when we were finally able to officially open it. It seemed fitting to invite Joan Ruddock, our Member of Parliament, and Peter Hall, the bishop of Woolwich, to open the park together. Church and government resources had come together to make this park possible. It was a happy day, full of celebration. The children laughed and posed for press photographers as they climbed on the climbing frame and belted down the slide. Even Joan Ruddock, MP, took a turn! I remembered Kevin bouncing on the mattress in this same spot two years before and quietly thanked God that we were able to do this for the children.

COMMUNITY LIFE at St. Michael's was easier to nurture than church attendance. People often measure the quality of a church, or indeed its minister, by the size of the congregation. If we had been judged according to that criterion, neither St. Michael's nor I would have been regarded as a great success. "You learn about failure in the inner city" was a phrase I used more and more frequently. Things that I knew worked in other churches never quite took off; events like house groups, where small groups met in church members' houses, were — rather like dinner parties — a middle-class practice.

The poor, inner-city church grows more slowly and has a distinctly different cultural identity to its middle-class counterparts. This has an upside. The culture of a small, inner-city church is much more down-to-earth, interactive, honest, and supportive. For example, it wasn't unusual for me to be interrupted in the middle of a sermon, or indeed any part of the service. One person might have a question to ask, another an opinion to express. It was often completely unrelated to what I was talking about, which was a challenge, and a good one. When the time came to pray, we would first of all have a time of sharing, where people had the freedom to say out loud the things that they were concerned about or needed prayer for. This made the prayers that followed much more meaningful, and they really belonged to the people.

Every member of St. Michael's was a unique character in one way or another. Hardly anyone could be described as being part of a stereotypical nuclear family; we had only one conventional family in the congregation, of a mum, dad, and two kids. For most of us, "family" meant something quite different, and not one personal situation was the same as another. Our small church was a family of sorts: when a member of our family died, we all grieved; when a new baby was born, we all rejoiced.

One parishioner, Rose, was schizophrenic and lived alone in one of the high-rise tower blocks. I spent a lot of time with her and grew to care for her deeply. She was sixty years old, and it was agony for her to hear the voices of women in her head, telling her to go out and prostitute herself on the streets. When she had very bad episodes, Rose would spend periods of time in the hospital, where her treatment would be monitored and her medication re-balanced. St. Michael's was Rose's family, and she knew that we loved her.

Another three elderly parishioners came from the Ludwick Mews sheltered housing on the estate. Michael, Marion, and Marjorie were affectionately known to all as "the three Ms." Michael had difficulty with his legs and walked with a cane. He was almost deaf and wore a hearing aid. Marion was certified blind and always brought a very thick magnifying glass with her to church. Dear Marjorie was in very good health. In her eighties, she looked after the other two, who were about fifteen years younger than her. It wasn't unusual for me to announce a hymn and then hear Michael shout, "What did she say?" Marion would flip through her large-print hymnbook, saying, "I can't find it," while Marjorie would be yelling the hymn number in Michael's ear and finding the right page for Marion. They reminded me of the three wise monkeys. Sadly, all of "the three Ms" have subsequently passed on, but it didn't surprise me that Marjorie outlived both Michael and Marion.

Two new people, Carrie and Phil, arrived at church one Sunday morning, looking for the woman curate they had read about in the newspaper. Carrie was about six months pregnant, and they had just moved into the neighborhood. In the years that followed, they threw themselves wholeheartedly into the life of the church and community, helping out where they could. When their son, Thomas, was born, the church was very excited: St. Michael's had a new baby. He would happily wander around from person to person, giving hugs and making faces. Then, a couple of years later, Gracie Rose was born. Carrie sat on St. Michael's management committee and became one of the founding members of the parent-and-toddler group.

Carrie and Phil were around my age, and I was grateful not only for their involvement but for their friendship. Amazingly, it felt like they had been called to St. Michael's or, to put it another way, that God had sent them. In my experience, that is rare. Christians often talk about how

God "called" them to this church or that, yet they always seem to be called to very nice, successful churches. I have hardly ever heard anyone say that God has called them to a small, struggling church in the inner city, which is in much greater need.

Our organist was sixteen-year-old David. He lived on the estate with his mum, Leslie, and both of them were extremely faithful members. David was extraordinarily gifted, and his mum often joked that she must have been given the wrong baby in the hospital. St. Michael's was very proud of David on the day he went off to university and managed to give him a small book grant each year. David may well have been the only kid from the estate to make it to university, and it wasn't just his mum who felt overwhelming pride and deep joy. The church missed David in many ways, not least because we were left without an organist. Thankfully, Phil played the guitar. With that and instruments from the nursery's music cart we usually managed to "make a joyful noise unto the Lord" — if not always tuneful.

There were many other people who made up the vibrant congregation and, most of the time, it was a sheer joy to be the minister there. Like a family, we shared in each other's fears, pain, and bereavement. But we also shared in each other's joys, laughed at each other's jokes, and together found hope. As a family, we found healing, learned new things about God and ourselves, nurtured and prayed for one another. In our lives as well as our worship, we praised God who gave meaning and direction to our lives.

The times it felt difficult for me at St. Michael's were when we had Holy Communion services. I was a deacon, not a priest, so Kim Hitch, the male vicar, had to come down onto the estate to celebrate Communion services, while I went to St. James to lead a "Family Service." St. Michael's loved to see Kim, and I enjoyed being with the congregation at St. James, but it made no sense that I was unable to conduct Holy Communion in the place where I was in effect the "priest" all through the week. It didn't make sense to the congregation either. One or another of them would often say, "If you can do our weddings, baptisms, and funerals, why do we need a man to come and say important words at the Eucharist?"

When, several years later, I was finally ordained a priest, I found Holy Communion to be the liturgical focus and climax of all the pastoral care that had gone on during the week. As I continued to minister at St. Michael's and struggle with the congregation toward the ordination of women, I knew that we all shared a sense of incompletion in this particular area. We looked forward to the day when a woman's liturgical ministry would be made whole.

Chapter Seven

Honest Women

When I was a little girl, there was a letter that I wrote with great care and precision each November. It was to Father Christmas and contained a list of the presents I hoped to receive. At some point in my childhood, I came to the crushing realization that there was no Father Christmas, but I kept up the pretense for as long as I could get away with it. I worked out that my letter to Father Christmas gave my parents and relatives an idea of what presents I wanted, so, one year, I carefully put at the top of my list the thing I wanted most with all my heart — a chemistry set.

As Christmas day approached, I got more and more excited about the fun I would have doing all kinds of interesting chemistry experiments. The presents were piled up around the tree and there were a few parcels that looked promising. When the day finally arrived, I could hardly contain myself.

There was a particularly cruel tradition in my family of postponing the opening of presents until after the queen's speech had been broadcast to the nation at 3:00 p.m. on Christmas Day. "Remember, darling, patience is a virtue," my grandma would say, as she settled herself down for a cup of tea with the queen.

Finally that Christmas, the speech was over. "Can we open the presents now? Can we?" Ray and I chorused.

We passed out the presents and then opened them one by one in turn. As each present was revealed, my excitement turned to disappointment as I realized that none of my presents was a chemistry set. I bit my lip and held back the tears bravely until my brother opened his last present from my uncle. Much to my horror, it was a chemistry set. I think it was probably the most miserable Christmas I'd ever had.

My experience as a woman in ministry, in that waiting period when women were not eligible for ordination to the priesthood, reminded me of the disappointment, anger, and frustration that I felt when my brother received the very thing that I had so desired. At the same time, I was reminded that prayer is no Christmas-list affair, and that it involves engagement, struggle, waiting, and trust. My faith in my family had been swiftly restored after that terrible Christmas. My birthday falls four days later, and, guess what . . . I got my chemistry set!

Before women could be ordained, it was our constant prayer that the church would recognize our calling and "make honest women of us." The road to priesthood for women was a long and winding one. The first woman ever to be ordained a priest in the Anglican Communion was the Reverend Florence Li Tim Oi in January 1944. She was a deacon and head of a girl's school in Hong Kong. It always amuses me that she was ordained to the priesthood by the bishop of Hong Kong and South China just before he and other male priests fled ahead of the Japanese troops. Clever!

In 1971, more women were ordained to the priesthood in Hong Kong, including the Reverend Joyce Bennett, the first English woman priest.

The American struggle for ordination was also interesting. We had all heard about the group of eleven women who were "irregularly" ordained priests in Philadelphia in 1974. I couldn't imagine the English women doing that and hoped that the whole Church of England, or at least a two-thirds majority of it, would come to a common mind and agree to ordain us as priests. I have always preferred to work within the structures of the church to bring about change and felt uneasy about the American protest.

In 1976, just two years after those "irregular" ordinations, the General Convention of the Episcopal Church in the United States voted in favor of women's ordination. For the American women, though, ordination was not limited to priesthood and, in 1989 Barbara Harris was consecrated as a bishop.

Other provinces of the Anglican Communion around the world were also debating the issue and ordaining women: New Zealand, Canada, Brazil, Kenya, Uganda, Cuba, Puerto Rico, and Ireland to name a few of them. The Church of England was among the last to change its four-hundred-year-old tradition.

My friends outside the church couldn't understand it. I was often asked, "Why is it taking so long to change? Why are some groups of people in the church so opposed to women being priests? What is their position?" The truth is that there were several theological positions. People were opposed to women being priests for a variety of reasons.

On occasion, I came face to face with opposition from a colleague who was firmly rooted in the evangelical wing of the church. Each year, on Good Friday, the churches around my parish in New Cross came together for a "march of witness" that ended with a united service in one of our churches. One year it was to be at my church, and I was preaching. The other churches were to share in different aspects of the service. Our small planning group had decided that the evangelical church with a youth group should be asked to take responsibility for the Bible readings, so I phoned the vicar.

"Ian, we wondered if your church would do the Bible readings at the Good Friday service? Perhaps the youth group could do a dramatic interpretation of the Scriptures?"

There was silence at the other end of the phone. Finally he said awkwardly, "Could you tell me who will be preaching?"

"I will be preaching," I said wondering what that had to do with anything.

"Well, in that case, I'm afraid our church won't be participating in the service," he said. I was confused. Had someone told him that I was a terrible preacher? Had I offended him in some way?

"Why exactly does the fact that I am preaching prevent you from being part of the service?" I asked.

"Well, it's nothing personal, but I don't believe that women should have any authority over men. I teach that in my church, and I'm afraid it would set a bad example to our young people if they saw you preaching."

I wasn't personally hurt or upset. I think the vicar really believed that it wasn't "personal." But I was angry at the kind of example *he* was setting and the teaching he was giving to vulnerable and trusting members of his congregation, both young and old.

For evangelical Christians, the Bible is the word of God and has absolute authority. But when it comes to interpretation, or discovering what certain passages were intended to mean, there is a wide range of opinions. Ian was definitely on the more conservative side. Some evangelicals read the teachings of St. Paul and take passages like those in Paul's first epistle to Timothy chapter 2, verse 12, literally, when he says: "I do not permit a woman to teach or to have authority over a man; she must be silent. For Adam was formed first, then Eve.... " This and other passages about women led the more conservative to argue that it was unbiblical for women to be in positions of headship. They were opposed to women being priests because women would soon be in positions of leadership and authority as they became appointed as vicars of churches.

Less conservative, more progressive evangelicals interpreted the same passages of Scripture, but took into account the context in which it was written and the culture it was intended to be applied to. They were supportive of women in ministry and leadership.

Many evangelicals have objections to the very nature of "ordination" and "priesthood" in the church. While these rites grew from early church tradition, they cannot be found in the New Testament exactly as we have institutionalized them today. One evangelical vicar said to me with great concern, "I wouldn't want to ordain you women into something that's not right." I replied, "You can hold that position with any integrity and consistency only if you first of all resign and then oppose the ordination of any more men to the priesthood as well."

At the other extreme of the Church of England are those who prefer a more Catholic style, the Anglo-Catholics. Scripture as the word of God is important to them, too, but so is tradition. Anglo-Catholics also had a number of different reasons why they were opposed

to women priests. Some saw the priest at the Holy Eucharist as the "Vicar of Christ," vicariously being Jesus.
One priest said to me, "Jesus was a man, so only men can
represent Christ at the altar." Well, there's logic for you.
I had to think about my response.

I replied, "Jesus was completely human, so he had to
be either a man or a woman. He couldn't be some hybrid
being that was both. In every mystical and spiritual sense,
he represented both men and women. He died for men
and women. He offers life to men and women. Surely
if we say that priests must be exactly like Jesus in his
humanity, then priests will have to be Jewish and people
of color as well as being male."

Other Anglo-Catholics feared that if the Church of
England ordained women as priests it would destroy any
hope of unity with the Roman Catholic Church. But there
is a bigger obstacle to this unity than the ordination of
women, and that is the question of the authority of the
pope. Agreement on this issue is difficult to imagine. In
addition, there is a growing movement at the grassroots,
parish level of the Catholic Church that longs for change,
and very many Catholic clergy and laity hope that one
day Roman Catholic priests will be allowed to marry and
Roman Catholic women will be accepted as priests.

The main objection to ordaining women, however, was
that the tradition of the church should not and could not
be changed. Jesus' twelve apostles were men, and they in
turn appointed men to continue the church. Through the
"laying on of hands" new leaders for Christ's church were
appointed successively. This practice of the early church
appointing its leaders eventually became known as "ordination" and the concept of "apostolic succession" became

an important tradition for both the Catholic and the Anglican Church. Anglo-Catholics believed that if women
were ordained the tradition of male apostolic succession
would be somehow broken, or at least changed and possibly tainted. The church would no longer be the church
that they were ordained into. One staunch, traditional-
ist priest, Father Geoffrey Kirk, founded a group called
"Forward in Faith." He once said, "It's not that we are
opposed to women priests. We simply don't believe it's
theologically possible for them to exist at all."

There were also a large number of Anglo-Catholics in
favor of the ordination of women as priests. They appreciated the value of tradition and the richness of Catholic
liturgy and spirituality, but at the same time were open to
change and renewal as the Spirit of God leads the church.
They were called "Affirming Catholics."

The labels were often confusing as were the issues, yet
I was glad to have the chance to contribute to the debate.
I wanted all of us to move to a place of greater understanding of each other's positions so that we would all be
in the most informed position to cast a vote.

Despite my frustration, I never became a campaigning
member of the Movement for the Ordination of Women
(MOW): it wasn't my preferred approach. I pursued the
same goal in a different way. I felt I could best bring about
change by working within the structures of the church,
using the gentle art of persuasion. It seemed to me that
some who had been put off by the more militant, feminist
approach would respond more positively to a less adver-
sarial approach. My chance to try that out came sooner
than I expected.

The whole of the Church of England was talking about
the ordination of women to the priesthood. Everyone

knew that it would be the job of the next General Synod
to make the decision "Yes" or "No." The Synod is the
governing body of the Church of England, with elected
lay and ordained representatives from all over the country. Elections for a new General Synod take place every
five years. The big issue for the 1990 elections was where
a candidate stood on the ordination of women. In order
for this democratic process to work well, it was important that everyone was well informed and understood
all angles of the debate. The bishops encouraged everyone, from church members in the pews to representatives
on deanery and diocesan synods, to be educated and
informed around the issue. When it came to electing representatives for General Synod, it was hoped they would
reflect the wishes of the whole church. Southwark diocese
was blessed with a well-equipped Lay Training Department. Marlene Hicken called me one day with a request.
"Joy, we want to put together a team to make a presentation to as many areas of the diocese as we can. I want you
and John Hall to help with this project. I've asked John
to present the various arguments against the ordination
of women, and I'd like you to present the arguments in
favor." It was the kind of challenge I liked. We had a year
before the elections took place to help people understand
the various positions within the church. We put together a
program, which we affectionately came to refer to as The
Road Show, and managed to address thirty-two different
deanery synods in that one year.

The historical context and the current situation in the
wider Anglican Communion were presented as an introduction. John and I would then each take our turn to
outline four or five of the main reasons why people were

either for or against the ordination of women to the priest-hood. When we were finished with our presentations, Marlene took questions of clarification. Then the people would discuss their feelings and views in small groups. When we gathered back together we heard and responded to questions and opinions from the whole group.

Our aim was to help people understand each other. It was important that we model a new way to debate the issue in a nonadversarial way. There were ground rules to try to make the evening helpful and informative. Destruc-tive anger and personal attack were to be avoided at all costs. We wanted people to be willing to listen to views that differed from their own without needing to knock them down. Too often debates on issues such as women's ministry, homosexuality, and abortion — to name but a few — are charged with powerful negative emotions and become shouting matches with each side vehemently de-fending their position. In such events, people rarely listen to each other or come to any place of new understanding.

The plan was for our presentations to be a much more positive experience for people on both sides of the de-bate as well as for those who were undecided. It helped that John Hall and I became good friends and that we were able to demonstrate that we could listen to and re-spect each other in these meetings. We found ourselves moving to a much deeper understanding of the other's position. So much did our appreciation of each other's views grow that, on one occasion, I found myself defend-ing John against a woman who accused him of being a misogynist. On another occasion, I was ill, and John pre-sented my side of the argument extremely convincingly in my absence.

By the end of the year, we were tired but extremely pleased that our road show had been so well received. We had successfully modeled a way not only to be respectful but also to be united in friendship with those with whom we disagreed.

I so enjoyed getting to know the whole diocese and speaking about the ordination of women that I was fairly easily persuaded to stand for election to General Synod. I understood that it was unlikely for such a young and newly ordained member of the clergy to be elected, but I decided that the experience of running would stand me in good stead for the future.

I wrote my manifesto, which was distributed to the six hundred clergy in the diocese. There were seven clergy seats allocated to Southwark Diocese and about twenty-five of us were in the running. I was nominated by Peter Price, a clergy friend who is now the bishop of Bath and Wells. I was seconded by John Hackett, a clergyman from Holy Trinity, Clapham. Sadly, John has since died.

After weeks of waiting and an agonizingly close count, I learned, to my great surprise and delight, that I had been elected. So, too, had John Hall. How had it happened? Still twenty-nine for a few more months, I would be the youngest member in the House of Clergy. I believe it was a combination of things that led my colleagues to give me their votes. After so much exposure in the road show, I was a name that clergy could put a face to and someone they knew could speak in debate. My manifesto was perceived to be a good one: it was clear, concise, and honest. I added my picture at the top too, just in case people remembered my face but not my name. I represented new blood, young energy, a commitment to the inner city and the marginalized . . . and, of course, I was a woman.

Meanwhile, back in the parish at St. Michael's, our staff was growing. A year after my appointment there, a new curate, Duncan, joined the team. Duncan was a wonderful colleague and soon became a great friend. He loved art and literature and used these and his great gifts as a teacher in many areas of ministry.

It was a potentially painful time for us when, after his first year as a deacon, he was to be ordained a priest. I would continue to be a deacon. Duncan asked me if I would read the Gospel at his ordination service. I thought about it for a while. I could either be angry that he, my junior colleague, was being made a priest and I was not, or I could joyfully celebrate his special day. To choose the former would have been hurtful to Duncan, and it wasn't his fault. I decided on the latter and agreed to read the Gospel. When we arrived at the church, there was the usual, faithful group of women standing on the steps in protest. They held banners that simply read, "Where are the women?"

As I sat in the church, as a deacon serving at Duncan's ordination, I pondered the situation. I was inside the church and the other women clergy were outside. This was an interesting picture.

I was, of course, in complete agreement with my colleagues protesting outside but was also happy to continue contributing to the movement by working from the inside.

In 1991, Kim Hitch took a new job as the rector of St. James's Team Ministry in Kidbrooke, which left Duncan and me to run the interregnum. "Interregnum" is a strange word that is Latin for "between reigns." So, the vicar/king had gone and we would eventually be given a replacement, but not for a year. It was a strange thing to be the senior member of staff with a curate who was a

Outside Church House with the bishop of Dover on the day that the General Synod voted to ordain women, November 11, 1992.

priest and able to do Holy Communion services when I was not. Fortunately, we were friends as well as colleagues and we worked well as a team, so there was no tension between us as we ran the parish together.

It was the following year, in November 1992, that the historic vote took place in the General Synod to ordain women as priests. It was by no means a foregone conclusion, and the day was full of tension and suspense. At the end of the debate, which lasted all day, the measure to allow women to be priests just passed by only one vote. It sounds incredibly close, and it was breathtaking, but that one vote actually gave a two-thirds majority in each of the voting houses, Bishops, Clergy, and Laity.

The celebration that followed was wonderful but not over the top. Those of us who had worked hard and waited long for this moment were indeed jubilant, but we were also sensitive to the feelings of those who were devastatingly disappointed on that day. Back in our churches as deacons, we would still have to wait for another two years before the first ordinations would take place in 1994.

Christmas was approaching. As one of the busiest times of the year for clergy, it was usually not until the afternoon of Christmas day that I could begin to unwind. That was until "CRISIS" came into the life of St. Michael's. Then the unwinding didn't start until several days later.

CRISIS is an organization well known for its "Open Christmas" — a temporary shelter for the homeless of London. In the two weeks over Christmas, when a lot of public facilities and spaces like libraries and shopping centers are closed, an enormous team of volunteers takes over a donated vacant warehouse and provides a comfortable and festive experience for thousands of people who need it. Clothing, good food, medical care, dentistry, hairdressing, TB screening, entertainment and even foot massages are some of the wonderful gifts brought every year by volunteers. Hundreds of mattresses are piled up around the room and laid down across the huge expanse of floor at night. The Open Christmas has become an increasingly popular and meaningful way for volunteers from all walks of life to spend their Christmas break and offer their talents and gifts.

It was November when I got my first call from the chair of CRISIS. "Reverend Carroll, we were wondering if you would be open to the church center at St. Michael's being an alternative Open Christmas shelter for women. Sometimes the women feel intimidated by the men or have different needs. We would like to expand what we offer and provide them with a smaller, more private space. If you were open to this, perhaps I could come and look around?"

After discussing how our space might work and getting approval from the church and center managers, we agreed to give it a try. Our building was ideal. The large gymnasium, complete with changing room and showers, was to be the main living area. The coffee bar area where the nursery usually was located became space for the volunteers. As soon as the nursery broke up for the Christmas holidays, the place was transformed for two weeks.

The site was to be "off the record" — a secret site where the women would feel safe from the guests at the main site. St. Michael's, tucked away in the middle of the Milton Court Estate, was ideal. A shuttle minibus was made available to transport guests and volunteers back and forth between sites several times a day if needed.

Two women, Freda and Wendi, coordinated the site. As the warden of the center and their host, I watched them work and witnessed their commitment. My respect for these two compassionate and capable women grew as quickly as our friendship did. I knew right away that I wanted to do more than witness this program: I wanted to be involved. Soon I was spending time with the women who came as guests as well as with the volunteers. The stories of how some volunteers came to be there were often as moving or heartbreaking as the stories of the guests.

Vera was one of many guests who struggled with mental illness. She had had a mastectomy some years before and believed that she had been wrongly treated by whoever had carried out her operation. She carried a bag full of evidence written on paper napkins. She was also convinced that the government was poisoning her in a number of different ways. Sometimes it was with poisonous gas, which affected only her as she traveled on the bus. This meant she wouldn't eat any hot food because of the damage she thought had been caused to her throat by the poisons. Vera was very particular as to what she could eat, and one thing she had to have was All-Bran. Late one Christmas Eve, for a bit of peace and quiet, the volunteers drove around to service station mini-marts to find her some.

I remember, too, the warm and smiling face of Mary. She loved to eat, but much of her food ended up all over her clothes. Mary also loved to talk, and it moved me to hear her life story.

She, too, had suffered mental illness for most of her life. Her own mother had lived and died in a hostel in Dublin. At an early age, Mary had given birth to two sons, both of whom were later adopted. She couldn't wait for them to reach the age of eighteen, when they would be free to search for her.

Not all the women at the shelter were technically "homeless." Edith, for example, attended the Open Christmas every year, always wearing a hat and carrying a traditional handbag. She had a husband whom she lived with but didn't speak to, and she spent her life attending different day centers in London. Edith was a staunch Christian and knitted hundreds of woolen squares to make blankets for charity.

Another of the guests gave us quite a surprise. Shortly after "Linda's" arrival, we discovered that "she" was a transsexual. She kept it a secret that she was still male as her mental state had not been stable enough for her to have the operation. She claimed to be pregnant, took folic acid regularly, and carried a baby doll with her all the time. The volunteers had to go and buy a shower curtain so that the other women wouldn't discover. Linda wore short skirts and wobbled on rather high heels and some mornings she had to use foundation make-up to disguise the fact that she had cut herself while shaving.

I was often reminded of how close so many people are to becoming homeless. It really doesn't take much bad luck to push someone who is just about coping with life over the edge into homelessness. Audrey was one such person. There had been a gas leak at her home that blew up her flat, leaving her very badly burned and scarred. She became a heavy drinker. I remember her being in her late forties and still having a beautiful singing voice.

I was a pastor, a listening ear, and a friend to those who needed me. One of the greatest needs I was able to meet was the volunteers' need for a quiet space and bedrooms to sleep in, in my flat upstairs. Shift leaders who finished work either early in the morning or late at night just had to crawl upstairs to take a bath, have a drink, unwind, or simply sleep.

What the guests liked was being able to treat the Women's Open as home. They could walk around in a nightdress all day if they really wanted to and, because the mattresses didn't have to be stacked at the Women's Open, they could even choose to stay in bed. Without the large numbers of men around, they were able to retain some of their dignity, have a cup of cocoa, and brush their teeth at night. The volunteers really tried to spoil the guests. Their beds were made with clean sheets and, in the mornings, they would give breakfast orders in bed. One volunteer came especially to give reflexology and massages to the guests and another to do hairdressing.

On Christmas Eve, the midnight communion service had a wonderfully different feel. The congregation gathered around the communion table. I assisted Kim, who took the service. As I handed out the bread and wine and repeated the familiar words: "The body of Christ," "The blood of Christ," I saw the faces of those gathered. They were a mixture of weathered, tired, sick, paranoid, trusting, and hopeful faces. It was a communion of the body of Christ that felt very authentic. Jesus Christ, who welcomed the outcasts and valued the undervalued, was there.

On Christmas Day, Freda and Wendi dressed up as Mother Christmas and her elf and distributed wrapped presents to each guest. Many gifts like toiletries, sweets, socks, and gloves had been donated and the guests were so grateful for so little. Special visitors included a traditional storyteller, a magician, and a circus-skilled artist. One regular visitor to the Open Christmas was the late dean of St. Paul's, Eric Evans. When he turned up the first year, one of the volunteers said to him, "You can't come in here...you're a man." He was eventually allowed in, although Vera was still convinced he was a government agent.

Chapter Eight

Immanuel

It was 1993 and General Synod was in its February session at Church House in Westminster. During the lunchtime break, I took the chance to visit the bookshops around the corner. Faith House was the more Catholic and "high church" of the two. Stepping through the doors was like stepping back in time. I always imagined there would be an ecclesiastical version of Scrooge serving behind the counter. There was, of course, no such person to be found, and they sold great church candles for a very good price. It was time to get stocked up, not just for church but also for my living room! As I wandered around, I felt slightly out of place. I supposed most of the staff and regular customers would be traditional Anglo-Catholics, opposed to the ordination of women. There I was, look-ing around, brazenly wearing my black shirt and clerical collar. I didn't want to be a source of discomfort but I did want the candles, so I bought them quickly and left.

Next, I entered the Church House Bookshop, which felt more welcoming. As well as finding books and resources, it wasn't unusual for me to bump into old friends there, or meet new ones. Bishops chatted with their clergy and laity as they lined up to pay for their books, and many a clerical gossip was to be had while browsing the shelves.

I was just about to leave with a new purchase when David Isherwood, the vicar of Immanuel, Streatham Common, came over to greet me. We talked for a while about the General Synod proceedings, which he had come to watch from the public gallery. Before long David shared with me that he was having difficulty filling a vacant position for a woman deacon at his church. I was ready for a move and wanted to work in partnership with another person or team. I had no personal need or ambition to be "in charge" of a church, but wanted to work collaboratively. "Tell me more about the parish and the kind of colleague you are looking for," I said. As he spoke, I knew that I wanted to hear more, but not in the bookshop.

David sounded like he was open to taking on an experienced woman deacon to work with, rather than under, him. "David, do you think I could be the kind of person you are looking for?" He looked surprised, and his eyes lit up. Just then I had to get back to the Synod. "Call me next week, and we'll talk some more," I said. "I need to think this through."

I had been at St. Michael's, on the Milton Court Estate, for five years. Church policy was that newly ordained clergy should stay for no more than four years in their first post. After that, some went on to be vicars in charge of a church of their own, some went on to be chaplains of hospitals, colleges, or prisons, and others would take on a second curacy acting as an assistant to the vicar. It would have been better for St. Michael's if I could have stayed longer, but I had no choice. I needed to gather a different kind of experience and had started looking around.

If women had been allowed to be priests at that time, I might have been persuaded to take a church of my own, but they weren't. I wanted to be in parish ministry, but I didn't want to be sidelined as someone's assistant. Curates were often given special areas of responsibility in the church — youth work or the lay training, for example — and were left to get on with it. I wanted to be in partnership as equally as was possible, sharing the whole broad range of parish ministry.

The more I spoke with David and explored the position available at Immanuel, the more interested I became. It was clear that David was eager to model a more radical style of partnership in ministry; he wanted an associate, not an assistant. We agreed that I would apply to be the "associate vicar," a title that designated a ministry together with an incumbent vicar, not on behalf of one.

I was interviewed and then warmly welcomed by the people of Immanuel, Streatham Common. On September 10, 1993, I moved into 98 Ellison Road, SW16. At the welcome party after my first Sunday service, several people gave short speeches. Betty, a long-time member and lay minister of the church said, "I am assured by people I know at the Maudsley Hospital that Joy is a very balanced person, and we are lucky to have her." Maudsley was the local psychiatric hospital, but I took it as a compliment!

It was exciting to discover my new neighborhood. It was very different from living and working on the housing estate in Deptford. When I was a teenager growing up in West Norwood, Streatham was the place to go for fun. The bowling alley, the ice rink, the cinemas, the nightclub (which as youngsters we knew as "The Cat's Whiskers") and the hundreds of restaurants made it a hive of activity.

The community was a real mix of people from a wide variety of backgrounds and income brackets. The challenge for the church was to reflect that variety in its membership as much as possible. Immanuel did a good job: it was the most socially, economically, and racially mixed church that I had come across, and I was delighted to be a part of it.

One of the wonderful features of London is its parks and commons. Streatham Common provided a welcome break in the urban sprawl that flanked the A23 Brighton Road. The church, with its square clock tower, was well situated on the other side of the main road, opposite the common, and boasted a wonderful view full of greenery and community activity. This view was most enjoyed by the staff and customers of the Beehive Community Cafe, what I liked to call the "shop front" of the church.

The Beehive was funded by the Church Urban Fund and was managed by a warm, down-to-earth, and very attractive member of our congregation called Jessica Williams. The café was a place where people could drop in for breakfast, lunch, a sandwich, or just a cup of tea. What people found when they came to the Beehive was a team of volunteers who worked with Jessica to provide listening ears, wise counsel, and friendly faces.

The Beehive's tables were cheerfully decked in gingham cloths, with china salt and pepper pots and plants. A delicious smell of cooking sausages and bacon would waft down the road and draw in passersby laden down with shopping from Sainsbury's, or people with nowhere to go who were starved for some warmth and care. A number of Beehive customers were the mentally ill residents of hostels in the neighborhood who were trying to come to terms with the lonely and often frightening implications

of the government's policy of "care in the community."
Some customers were pensioners, some were homeless,
and some were unemployed. Many were mums and children who had been using the parent-and-toddler group
we ran in the hall, and others were local workmen who
liked the atmosphere.

The Beehive was a fabulous place, and I spent as much
time there as I could. For a while, I even helped run
it when Jessica was unavailable. Every morning after
prayers, David and I would move on into the Beehive for
a cup of tea and a snack. It was the perfect spot for us to
be available and accessible to the people of the parish.

Immanuel was a lively and active church with many
natural links to the community around. Our closest link
was with our church primary school. A dedicated and
committed staff led the school and the education it offered to the neighborhood's children was second to none,
including expensive private alternatives. The inspectors
called it "an oasis of tranquillity within a busy urban
environment." Arthur Williams, the head teacher, was a
regular and active member of the congregation. He was a
thoughtful, consistent, and wise man, who was loved and
respected by parents and children alike.

Whenever I spent time with Arthur, he loved to tell me
about the funny things that children had said to him or to
one of the teachers. He told me of a science test where a
seven-year-old, when asked to explain why half the world
was in darkness and half in light, wrote "because God is
fair and everybody must have a turn." On another occasion, when Arthur was on playground duty, a group of
children marched up to him.

"Ben won't play fairly," they complained.

"What is he doing?" asked Arthur.

"He isn't obeying the rules," they replied.

"What are the rules?" asked Arthur.

"We have all gone to Mars on our spaceship. Ben is the captain, and he won't let us back to earth!"

Sometimes it was the parents who made us smile. One father wanted to impress on Arthur how seriously he took his role as a disciplinarian, and told him he used "capital punishment"!

As a former teacher who thoroughly enjoyed being with children, I found my "kid fix" at Immanuel. I visited the school often, led the occasional assembly, cheered at sports day, and enjoyed the excellent concerts and various school productions. The school choir and steel band were first-class, and we used them whenever possible at special church services and events. As one of the school governors, I tried to offer as much practical and pastoral support as I could to parents, children, and staff.

IT HAD BEEN TWO YEARS since the General Synod voted in favor of ordaining women. The houses of Parliament had also given approval, and the time had finally come for us to be ordained as priests. On the Tuesday before the ordination services, all the women to be ordained gathered in Southwark Cathedral for a rehearsal. Saturday was to be a wonderful but long and exhausting day for Bishop Roy Williamson. He was ordaining eighty women in Southwark Diocese alone and there were three identical services for each of the Episcopal areas of Croydon, Kingston, and Woolwich. Someone commented that it was a bit like a Moonie wedding!

Once the women had walked through the order of service, we boarded a bus taking us to the High Leigh Conference Center for our preordination retreat. Being

together with so many other women clergy for three days
was inspiring. I had been a deacon for only six years, but
many of the women I was on retreat with had been in
ministry for many more. They had first of all been called
"lady workers," then "deaconesses," which were both
lay orders. Then, in 1987, when the Synod agreed that
women could be admitted to the Holy Order of Deacon,
they were finally recognized as clergy.

I was especially thrilled to be there with my old high
school Religious Education teacher, Sylvia Martin, who
had been one of those faithful servants waiting and working for many years. I must have had the image of all these
fine women in my head when I said, "For every thousand
men who leave the church because of the ordination of
women, there's a thousand good women waiting to step
into their shoes." This was printed by the *Independent*
newspaper as one of their quotes of the week.

On Saturday, May 21, 1994, I and twelve hundred
other women were ordained to be priests in the Church
of England. The ordination service itself was glorious and
majestic. Processing down the aisles of the cathedral, surrounded by all of our friends and family, was incredibly
moving. I have always loved Southwark Cathedral. It is
small compared to most, but beautiful. I regularly volunteered to be the "cathedral chaplain for the day," just so
that I could enjoy the cathedral for a prolonged period
of time.

At the actual moment of ordination, the bishop laid
his hands on the candidate's head. He was joined by a
group of priests chosen by the candidate and all of them
together ordained the new priest. I was particularly glad
that my dad could be one of four chosen priests to share
in my ordination. As I knelt before Martin, the bishop of

The ordination of women meant I was finally able to celebrate Holy Communion – the focus of pastoral care.

Kingston, I tried to let the importance of what was about to happen sink in. The bishop began to speak the words of ordination and the priestly hands were planted firmly on top of my head. I believe they had all been instructed to press hard, and I felt well and truly ordained.

The welcome that I received at Immanuel the next day was warm and enthusiastic. Friends came from my previous parish in New Cross, and the church was full. On occasions like this, we opened the partition doors at the back of the church and the congregation overflowed into the church hall. I was to celebrate my first Communion as a priest and was incredibly nervous. I had sat through thousands of Holy Communion services, watching my male colleagues do what I was about to do, and yet I felt sick with fear — or perhaps it was anticipation. I'd stuck Post-It notes all over the big altar-service book, and there were pencil marks in the margins. I really wanted to get it right and celebrate Communion well.

David preached a fine sermon, and now the focus was on the bread and the wine as people listened to my female voice speaking the words of consecration that were so familiar. "On the night before he died, he took the bread and gave you thanks." I lifted the bread dramatically and my heart was pounding. "This is my body, which was given for you. . . . " When it came to holding up the chalice of wine, my hands were shaking, and I was afraid that I might spill it. "This is my blood which was shed for you and for many for the forgiveness of sins. Drink this all of you in remembrance of me."

As I administered the bread and wine to those who came to stand around the altar, I was powerfully aware that the focus here was on the body and blood of Christ, our spiritual food and drink, and not on me. I was honored to be the priest who consecrated it and gave it to the gathered people. That day all of us celebrated that women were no longer prevented from being priests simply because they were women. Now I could continue on with the job that God had called me to do, but do it as a priest.

THERE WAS ONE PART of ministry that I especially enjoyed. Greenvale nursing home was built beside Streatham Common to accommodate some of the patients who had been cared for in Tooting Bec Hospital before it was closed down. Many of the residents had Alzheimer's disease and were in need of full-time nursing care.

One day I received a call from a staff person at the newly opened home. "We wondered if you would mind coming in to visit from time to time. We would like our residents to have as much contact with others in the community as possible, and many of them were church-goers at one time." I discussed a plan with others from Immanuel, and we decided to hold regular services of Holy Communion there on the first Sunday afternoon of every month.

Being a priest and celebrating Holy Communion in the nursing home was a powerful and moving experience for me. I was often reminded of the deep significance and power of the consecrated bread and wine, and it became more important to all of us as each month went by. Each time we arrived, the residents would gather in the very pleasant lounge. They sat comfortably on easy chairs, and some lay on the couch, exposing large incontinence underwear, and seemingly unaware of what was going on. It was often noisy. One lady would be crying, saying her daughter never came to see her; she couldn't remember that her daughter had just been with her that very morning. Another man would shout at his friend because she wouldn't hold his hand. It was always difficult to get started, but wearing my white cassock alb helped them to realize that something religious was about to happen.

I would begin by laying a simple table with a white cloth, a chalice of wine, and a paten of wafers. I prepared very large-print hymn sheets each month, making sure to use only very well known and traditional hymns. David, our organist, and his wife, Marion, were fabulously committed to this ministry. David would play the piano, which was actually on the other side of glass doors in the conservatory, so he had to bang out the tune as loudly as he could so that we could hear him. Sadly, David couldn't always hear us and we would end up singing half a verse behind the tune of the piano! Marion and a few others who came from church would hand out hymn sheets, the confession, and the Lord's Prayer. Then one of them would read a Bible verse from those we had heard in church that morning. I would say just a few words about the reading, keeping it very simple and short, and then go

on to say a shortened version of the Prayer of Thanksgiving for the bread and wine before administering it to
those gathered.

It was a moving, and sometimes amusing, time. So
many of the congregation were confused, had lost their
ability to remember or to make the right connections, but
somehow the liturgy, the hymns, the confession, and the
Lord's Prayer soothed them and ministered deeply to their
souls. There were occasional flashes of recognition. An
old man who had trouble putting words together would
recite the Lord's Prayer with ease. Depressed residents
would sing out the hymns with gusto and — much to
David's consternation — at great speed. The bread and
wine became more powerful symbols than ever as these
physical elements hardly needed words to evoke deep spiritual awakenings. "The body and blood of Christ" were
words I often said with tears in my eyes as I dipped the
wafer into the wine and placed it in each person's mouth.

We also had our funny moments. I came to realize that
many of the residents receiving the wafer dipped in wine
needed me to actually direct them to open their mouths.
I would often say, "The body and blood of Christ, open
your mouth." They would dutifully do so, and in would
go the wine-soaked wafer. With one man I had the same
exchange of words every month. It went like this:

"The body and blood of Christ, open your mouth."

"No, no! Go away. I'm Church of England!" he would
shout. "I am Church of England too," I would reply
loudly. "Open your mouth!"

He would then do so, and all would be well. It must
have been confusing to him that a woman was giving him
Holy Communion.

Like children, people who suffer from Alzheimer's will often say what is on their mind without any concern for what is proper, polite, or appropriate. Often I had to hold back a giggle or find an appropriate response when I was heckled and interrupted midstream. Sometimes I was mistaken for the Virgin Mary or Princess Diana and, on one occasion, when I offered "the body and blood of Christ," the response was "Fuck off!" It was a ministry that warmed my soul and kept my feet firmly on the ground.

On the other side of Streatham Common, next door to the church, was St. John's, a Shaftsbury Society residential home for the elderly. Some of the residents were relatives of church members and quite a few of them — even wheelchair users — were regular church members themselves. One parishioner, Vera, a single, middle-aged woman, dedicated most of her life to the care of her family and friends, many of whom were elderly and at St. John's. She had a big heart and a humble spirit and always made sure that anyone who wanted to come to church was collected and taken back to St. John's afterwards.

Vera had a grand group of ladies who helped her. One of them, Florrie, was a faithful woman of God. She loved to read her Bible and prayed regularly for the needs of others. One day she was in the hospital recovering from surgery. The doctor stood at the end of her bed as she began to wake up from the anesthetic. She was confused as she emerged from her deep sleep. She opened her eyes, looked at the doctor in his white coat, and said, "Hello, God, I'm Florrie Shaw." When I was told about this, two things moved me. First, Florrie was so humble that she felt it necessary to introduce herself to God — as if God wouldn't know exactly who she was. Second, she was sure of where she was going if she *had* died. When Florrie did eventually die, the minister who conducted her funeral told that story. We were blessed to have great women such as this in our midst.

Most clergy feel weighed down by the expectation that they should visit everyone in the parish personally, whether they need a visit or not. My first boss, Kim Hitch, called this "tea-and-jam" visiting, and I think he rightly considered it a waste of valuable time. Of course, some visiting is really important but can't and shouldn't be the sole responsibility of the vicar. Immanuel was a church full of people with gifts, and I wanted the whole church to take a share in the visiting and pastoral care of the parish. I put out a call for a team of visitors. We had a number of training evenings and a group of about twenty people were willing to give it a try.

The group met monthly at my house on a Wednesday night. I collected a list of people who, for one reason or another, needed a visit from the church. Some of them were follow-ups from funerals I had conducted maybe six months before: bereaved partners who needed some-one to talk to. Others were elderly people who used to come to church but were now housebound. Then there were people who had visited the church once or twice and asked for a visit. Some were suggestions from members of the congregation who knew which of their neighbors might for some reason appreciate a visit.

In the week preceding the visiting evening, I would telephone the people we intended to see and have a con-versation with them over the phone, offering a visit from two members of the church on Wednesday night. Lots of people were thrilled to be called but declined the visit; it always seemed to work out that we had just the right

The documentary *Not the Vicar of Dibley* helped encourage the acceptance of women priests, yet still portrayed me as "myself."

number on the visiting team for those who said yes for that night.

When the team arrived at my house, I would put people in pairs and assign the visits. The "number one" visitor in the pair was the leader and would initiate and direct the conversation when visiting. The second visitor might be someone who had never visited before or felt nervous about being anything more than a support; these "number two" visitors often turned out to be most appreciated by the person being visited. The pairs would disperse, leaving behind another group in the visiting team who didn't actually go out but stayed behind to pray for those who did. After an hour or so, everyone would return to my house for refreshments and we would listen to each pair tell how their visit had gone. At the end we would all pray for everyone who had been visited that night.

We always felt encouraged and uplifted at the end of visiting nights. People often said things like, "I thought I was going visiting to do good for someone else, but I felt so moved and touched by the person I visited tonight." It was a two-way process of meeting Christ afresh. I also loved the visiting program for its inclusivity. The team was open to everyone in the congregation, and two of our mentally ill members always came. I once or twice sent them out as "number two" visitors, but usually they happily stayed behind to pray. The success of the visiting program was exciting and substantially reduced the stress of not getting enough visiting done.

David and I worked well together and I was grateful for his efforts to treat me as an equal partner in the ministry at Immanuel. We shared the parish work, including baptisms, weddings, and funerals. On Sundays we took turns in celebrating Holy Communion. We also worked with a great team of "readers." These were members of the congregation who had completed a rigorous theological training over a period of two years and were licensed to preach and teach. We had three readers who were included in the rota to preach at either the morning or evening services.

Twice a year, David and I would retreat for a day to pray for the parish and plan for the coming months. These were such valuable times to support one another as colleagues and encourage each other as friends. We laughed easily together and found that everything worked best if not taken too seriously.

One Sunday morning David and I were greeting people in the church foyer. As well as our usual church members a smattering of about fifteen visiting teenagers scurried in. I asked David, "Where have they come from? Is there some kind of camp or event for youth happening in Streatham?" Sometimes, when Carter's Steam Fair* was based on the common, we would have a crowd of folk from the fair come to worship with us. But I couldn't place this group of teenagers. David mumbled and shrugged his shoulders. Later on in the service, I had just finished making announcements and asked if anyone else had anything to announce. David stood up. "I wonder if our visitors could stand up so that we can welcome you." The teenagers stood up.

"Joy, would you please take a good look at these young faces and tell me if you recognize them." David led me to the front of the podium. I was very confused. I looked at the faces of the teenagers. They looked familiar but new to me. My mind must have been working very hard. All of a sudden I began to see who each of these young people were. "James, Lucy, Alison, Bunsie, Diptie, Matthew, Joseph!" These were the five-year-olds that I had taught at Gonville Primary School. They had organized a reunion and decided to surprise me by visiting Immanuel Church. David had been in on the plan and helped to make it work perfectly. We had a wonderful time afterwards, looking at photographs and sharing our memories of ten years before. I was so thrilled and proud to hear that they were all doing so well. Some had great plans to go to college or university. It didn't seem possible that I had helped them learn how to write their names. One of those boys still keeps in touch with me even now and, as I hear each year of his exploits and development, I feel very, very old!

---

*An antique amusement park where rides are steam powered.

In October 1995, David moved on to be the rector at Holy Trinity, Clapham Common. I was sorry to see him go, but glad for the chance to be the priest in charge. I never felt that I was left to run the parish on my own, however. The congregation at Immanuel was an incredibly gifted, energetic, and enthusiastic bunch. Everything we did involved a big team effort. This always filled me with admiration. How do people find the bigness of heart, the willingness to help, to do their bit for the church when they do it all in their spare time and don't get paid a penny for it? Jim Drury, a local plumber, was an amazing example of a man who did everything, from organizing church social events to handing out hymnbooks and welcoming people on a Sunday morning, and so much more in between.

Jim was always there on the Saturday in mid-December when we decorated the church for Christmas. Four or five others came too, including the church's wardens, Jenny and Martin, and Tracy who helped to keep the church clean. We would get down the old boxes from the church tower storeroom, blow off the dust, and begin the job. One year, Tracy suddenly yelled, "What about the Christmas tree, we haven't got a tree!" "Well," I said, "last year we bought a tree from Sainsbury's. Let's go and see what they've got." So off Tracy and I went, to choose a tree.

Sainsbury's is situated right next door to the church, and we enjoyed a good relationship. We provided them with after-church shoppers on Sundays (much to the consternation of those opposed to shops being open on Sundays), and Sainsbury's gave us a beautifully fresh-baked loaf for our Communion service every week. Norman, the manager, was always keen to know how I was doing and often remembered church projects and our school in his charitable donations. I loved going to the supermarket. It would take me several hours to do my shopping, as I would bump into so many parishioners who loved or needed to chat, and Norman was no exception.

That day, Tracy and I walked through the parking lot and looked around the back for Christmas trees but — what rotten luck — they had decided not to sell Christmas trees that year. Just at that moment, who should wander by but Norman. "Good morning, Vicar. How are you doing?" he asked.

"Norman," I replied with a grin, "we came to buy a tree for the church and you haven't got any, so we'll have to take our business elsewhere!"

"Hang on a minute there, Vicar, come with me." Norman led us into the entranceway, where they had an enormous and beautifully decorated tree on display for the season. He called over three of his lads on the staff, unplugged the lights, and said, "Boys, take this tree, go with the Vicar, and plug it back in, in the church. Off you go!" We all looked at him open-mouthed. "Are you serious?" said Tracy. He was. I gave Norman a big hug. "Thanks so much, this is fantastic!"

It was quite a sight to see three of Sainsbury's lads carrying a fully decorated Christmas tree down the main street and into the church! Jim and the team decorating the church could hardly believe their eyes.

BEING A MEMBER of the Church of England's General Synod continued to be a source of stimulation and education for me. Not only was I able to represent my parish, deanery and diocese and take their concerns to the debating chamber; I was also able to relay back to them decisions made by and issues facing the Synod. I made a number of speeches as a Synod member. I was always nervous but worked hard not to let it show, and I spoke in a number of debates on issues ranging from prison reform to homelessness.

The Synod met three times a year, twice in Church House, Westminster, and once at York University for several days in July. With most of the Synod members living on campus, this group of sessions always felt more relaxed and informal. The atmosphere was often jovial, and there was more time to build friendships and to network; much "business" was done in the university's bars each night.

It was during one of our York Synods that the Church Urban Fund wanted to highlight the plight of the homeless. The issue was being addressed in debate and we wanted to draw the nation's attention to the problem as well. A sponsored sleep-out was organized and, for one night, I — and a good number of fellow clergy and bishops — slept in cardboard boxes for the night. It was the middle of the summer, and our cardboard boxes were new and clean; there was no way we were re-creating the harsh reality of sleeping on the streets. We did, however, provide the press with some good photographs of bishops sleeping in boxes that went with the story we wanted them to write. Despite the lack of sleep, it was quite enjoyable — just for one night you understand! Events like this, and the fact that people had time to walk and talk together, fostered more of a sense of collegiality and unity at York than could be experienced in Westminster.

One morning I had an embarrassingly close encounter with a senior clergy member of the Synod. We were accommodated in student rooms in the residence halls, and none of them had private bathrooms. We became accustomed to keeping a lookout along the corridor for times when the shower became vacant. Clutching my wash-bag and towel, I scurried along the hallway one morning to the shower. Inside, I undressed and hung my clothes on the back of the door. When I had finished my shower, I wrapped my towel around me, grabbed my clothes and ran back to my room. As soon as I closed my door, however, I realized that I had left my panties hanging up on the shower door. I looked down the corridor and was about to make a dash to retrieve them when, to my horror, I saw the clergyman jump in to take his shower. I hoped that he would either not notice them or would politely leave them for me to retrieve when he had gone. But, no, a few minutes later there was a knock on my door. I opened it and there he was, gingerly holding my underwear between his finger and thumb. "Do these by any chance belong to you?" he asked with a grin.

Chapter Nine

Flying Bishops

On November 11, 1993, Richard Curtis, writer of *Four Weddings and a Funeral* and *Notting Hill,* sat in the public gallery of Church House, Westminster. The gallery looked down onto the circular chamber where the General Synod of the Church of England met for four days, twice a year. There was often a smattering of visitors who had a special interest in the debate that day. Even some Synod members liked to sit in the gallery from time to time, as it offered a great view of the proceedings and participants.

Richard was working on a new creation. He had written one episode of a new situation comedy for the BBC called *The Vicar of Dibley.* It was in its early stages, and he decided to talk to a real woman priest as he developed the character. What was life really like for women in the church? What were the issues they dealt with? Richard had already asked the great comedienne Dawn French to be the star of the show. He wanted to find a woman priest whom he and Dawn would both be able to relate to and understand.

"I was very keen not to write a fictional character that I was making up," said Richard, "but actually to have a contemporary person with the same frame of reference. Someone who knew about pop music and films and things like that, as I did. I wanted someone who'd been brought up in the same atmosphere of tolerance and punk, or whatever it was."

He therefore made his way to the General Synod meeting at Church House in Westminster, the heart of the Church of England. It was there that he heard me speak on the controversial subject of "Flying Bishops." The Church of England's decision to ordain women into the priesthood had not ended the controversy. For one, it prompted an exodus of nearly three hundred male clergy from the church; these men were able to claim generous compensation packages from the Church Commissioners. Those clergy and laity who objected but stayed in the church still felt that the church would be violated by the ordination of women. They pushed for special provisions to be passed, particularly in the area of Episcopal care; specifically, they wanted especially designated bishops who never had nor would ordain a woman. These bishops were to be called "Provincial Episcopal Visitors," but would become known as "Flying Bishops" because they flew from diocese to diocese, but had no diocese of their own.

In November 1993, exactly one year after the vote to ordain women to the priesthood and four months before it would actually happen, the Act of Synod regarding these special bishops was presented for approval. The Act would make it possible for two bishops to be consecrated specifically to care for those clergy and congregations who were opposed to the ordination of women. One was for the northern province of York and one for the southern province of Canterbury. All ordinations, confirmations, and other Episcopal duties needed by those in opposition to women priests would be performed by one of these two men.

The positions for and against the ordination of women were to be respected as positions of integrity and were called "the two integrities." Such language was encouraged to maintain a unity that was becoming increasingly fragile. The small group of twenty-five clergywomen on Synod, who were particularly sensitive to this need, held a meeting the day before the debate. I was the youngest among these women and had great respect for their wisdom and experience. One of them was a softly spoken, serene woman, of stature in her diocese, who exuded a grounded and mature spirituality. She said, "Well, we have what we wanted: we are to be ordained as priests. I think we need to be gracious to those who are hurting and vote for the Act of Synod. Let them have their bishops." There was a murmur of agreement around the room. I felt confused and torn. What she said really sounded like the kind thing to do, and it would indeed be gracious. But it didn't feel like the right thing to do. "Where is the theological integrity?" I thought to myself. "How can we create a system that is based on the assumption that bishops who have ordained women are somehow tainted?" I wanted to be kind and gracious, but I also wanted to maintain my integrity. I went home to sleep on it.

The next morning I got on the train at New Cross for my twenty-minute commute to Westminster. As I looked around at my traveling companions, most of whom were people of color, a new thought came to me. I believed that ordaining women was absolutely the right and just thing to do. Just as I believed that it was absolutely right for black people to be able to be ordained as priests. What if our debate today was about providing care for those opposed to the ordination of black people? Would the Synod want to be so gracious about it? I would certainly hope not. In that moment I decided to vote against the Act of Synod. I pulled out my notebook as the train chugged slowly into London and began to write what I knew I had to say in the debate.

When the chair of Synod called on me to speak, I could hardly believe it. I was incredibly nervous and my voice shook, but I hadn't felt so strongly about anything for a long time. I shared some of my struggle in the speech and finished with these words: "I have agonized about what is the most holy thing to do. Is it to be generous at all costs? Or is it to be true to a God of integrity and justice? In the end, I have decided to vote against the Act. What I am voting against is inconsistency and bad theology. I fear that the church may find herself bent so far backwards that she might fall over." I sat down to hearty applause. Sadly, the Act was passed, but not I believe without a heavy heart. With the benefit of hindsight, many more now agree that the Synod made a big mistake that day.

Richard Curtis heard my impassioned speech from the gallery and decided that I was the woman priest he was looking for. Perhaps he saw someone who looked a little like Dawn French and was around the same age. What-ever the reason, he looked up my telephone number and went away feeling pleased.

Synod meetings last three or four days and, by the end, I was always exhausted. Often I went home with a mi-graine, only to find several messages on my answering machine from journalists who wanted an interview about women priests. Usually I would oblige, believing it to be a good thing to nurture a positive relationship with the press. However, the demands of the press were invading the time I needed to do my job as a priest. Reporters from the *Sun* newspaper had, on one occasion, actually chased my colleague Judie and me around Westminster, trying to persuade us to talk to them for their report on "Vicars in Knickers"! I even received what felt like an almost abusive call from the editor of the *Sun*, accusing me of great snobbery for not taking this once-in-a-lifetime opportunity to communicate with the working-class and ordinary people of England.

It was therefore easy for me to get home and ignore any messages that sounded like yet another reporter. If they were that interested, they would call again: I wasn't about to spend precious time calling reporters back. Richard had left several messages on my answering machine, describing himself as a writer who wanted to talk to me. I ignored them. Later my friends laughed at me because I had no idea who Richard Curtis was. I soon discovered that he was the respected and well-known writer of *Mr. Bean* and *Black Adder* and the brains behind Comic Relief. Fortunately, Richard was persistent and, when he finally got the chance to explain his latest project to me, I couldn't resist his invitation to get involved as a friendly advisor to the team.

One morning a few weeks later, I was expecting two famous guests. The doorbell rang, and there stood Dawn French and Richard Curtis. Any nervousness I felt about meeting them was quickly dispelled as Dawn handed over a box of goodies, insisting that we couldn't work without chocolate cakes. In that first meeting with Dawn, I got to know a little about the woman who so easily makes people laugh. She is warm and funny, with a gift for putting people at their ease. As we talked, I found her to be sensitive and intelligent. She had a real desire to understand what made me tick and what it meant for me to be a priest. She asked about my calling to ordained ministry, and she wanted to know the reasons not only why I wanted to be a priest but, more fundamentally, why I was a Christian in the first place. I sensed that she was a deeply spiritual person, perhaps even a person of faith.

Richard listened intently and asked his own questions about the joys and frustrations of ministry. For example, how was it that I maintained a sense of self while in the role of priest? I told him about the things that energized me in the job and the things that drained me; the things that made me laugh and those that made me cry. He noticed little details about my life, like a mug I had in the kitchen with the inscription "Lead me not into temptation, I can find it myself."

When I first watched the program, I was delighted to see that he had portrayed Geraldine, the vicar, as absolutely human and quite vulnerable. One lovely touch, showing that he really picked up the identity question, was on the wall above the vicar's desk: a picture of Jesus and next to it a picture of Mel Gibson!

Richard and I spoke regularly, and he soon became a friend, while Dawn came back alone several times to talk more. On one occasion she came to watch me conduct a funeral. She parked her lovely sports car outside my house and traveled with me in my little red Ford Fiesta, as we wanted to be sensitive to the bereaved family and didn't want them to be aware of her presence. It was actually very funny to have Dawn French sitting at the back, pretending to be the organist's assistant, bending over the organ with a floppy hat covering her face. No one ever knew she was there, except the organist, of course,

To the press, I'm sure I'll always be known as "The Real Vicar of Dibley."

who was thrilled to take Dawn's autograph home to his granddaughter!

The first time I saw Dawn French as the vicar of Dibley, I was quite taken aback, as were many who knew me well. She had cut her hair the same as mine, wore the same kind of clothes, and actually had taken on some of my characteristics. My family always tease me for the way I ask: *"Did* you?" or *"Have* you?" or *"Do* you?" in response to someone — especially a child — telling me something about themselves. And here was the vicar of Dibley using the same pastoral phrases! Even the walls of the vicarage were painted in the same green and pink painted on my living room walls. In just a few meetings with me, Dawn had done her homework. Her great acting ability and Richard's clever writing had created a character that was sometimes uncomfortably close to home. Geraldine fell in love with the producer of *Songs of Praise,* got involved with politics, and ate far too much chocolate. My totally balanced and competent friend Ruth, who shared my house for four years, got rather worried when people asked if "Alice, the verger" was based on her!

The part of Geraldine was a particular challenge for Dawn because she was used to the characters she played being victims of ridicule. People were usually supposed to laugh at her characters, but with *The Vicar of Dibley* it was different. At first, Dawn wasn't sure how to make the program funny when she wasn't the source of comedy. She adapted brilliantly, and her looks of bemused exasperation were the kind of real emotions that many clergy found very funny because they reflected their own experience as pastors. The television audience, in general, also loved the new vicar. They found her warm, genuine, approachable, and the kind of person they would like as their parish priest.

I went to watch the program being filmed at the television studios, where I was shown around the set. I expected the actors to be preoccupied and busy, but each of them made time to say hello and show interest in the work and life of the "real vicar of Dibley." It was a happy and pleasant team who enjoyed making the episodes.

The "blessing of the animals" episode was especially fun as it was filmed on location in a little Oxfordshire village. There were animals everywhere, as local people had brought their own animals along to be extras, and an atmosphere of chaotic excitement ruled throughout the day. I stood behind the camera while it filmed people bringing their pets to church. In the episode, one member of the congregation is a tattooed punk with a dog named Satan. The vicar, Geraldine, pats Satan on the head and says, "very brave of him to come at all really. . . . " That day, Dawn had to welcome streams of people and animals filing into church, and then had to do it again, and again, and again. Soon the welcoming smile was wearing a little thin, and I wondered if she might be getting more insight into the role of a real vicar who shakes those hands over and over every week!

In another episode, Geraldine gets depressed and eats hundreds of chocolate bars. She wakes up in the morning with a stomach ache, surrounded by a sea of empty wrappers. To film that scene they had to unwrap hundreds of Crunchy bars, and guess who got to take them home for the kids at church?

To promote *The Vicar of Dibley,* many of the TV guides and entertainment sections of newspapers ran stories about how *The Vicar of Dibley* was based on a real woman priest working in the inner city of South London. It was a wonderful opportunity for me to talk about the work of the church in Streatham and to present a positive image of women in the church.

The series itself helped as England began the process of receiving women priests into its communities and churches. The vicar of Dibley was an intelligent, com-passionate, caring character with human frailties and vulnerabilities: that is what made the series work. She was a humanly saintly character, trying to pastor a rather odd group of parishioners. Many of my women colleagues commented on how the series seemed to have made them more approachable and accepted by the people they worked among.

I believe that in *The Vicar of Dibley* people saw a priest concerned for the weak and powerless. They saw a priest who wasn't afraid to stand up to the local councilor; a priest who was unafraid to put a clear glass window in the church and send the money raised for stained glass to the poor. Whatever she did, she was on the side of the people who needed her. She became their encour-ager and champion — rather like Jesus. That was what people liked.

Chapter Ten

Not the Vicar of Dibley

I snapped the strap of my helmet under my chin, grabbed a pile of letters that needed to be mailed, threw my rucksack over my shoulder, and wheeled my bike out through the front door. I often cycled around the parish. When the weather was good, it was so much easier than driving and parking the car. On my bike I would call greetings to people I recognized and could easily stop to chat with parishioners I met along the way. Children playing in the school playground would call and wave to me as I cycled by. Elderly ladies would chuckle and tut, saying that I looked more like a teenager than a priest in her thirties.

Today, I was off to have lunch with my friend, Martin, from the Church Urban Fund. Martin wanted to introduce me to film producer Marilyn Wheatcroft, who was interested in making a documentary about the Fund and some of its projects. "Joy, you would be a good person for Marilyn to meet and talk to," said Martin. "You have been directly involved with a couple of projects that CUF has funded. Come and tell her what a great thing it is. I'm even hoping you might be involved in making the documentary."

"I'll be there," I'd promised.

I locked my bike to a lamppost outside the restaurant in Norbury where we had agreed to meet and went inside. Martin introduced me to Marilyn, and we began to talk. I liked her: she was clever, interesting, and ran her own television workshop, creating and producing films and documentaries for the BBC. She listened as I described the after-school club based at St. Michael's on the Milton Court Estate. I described the children, and she loved hearing stories of how the club had changed the quality of their lives. I enthused about the Church Urban Fund and how the whole church felt a part of it. I also told her about the Beehive Café at Immanuel and invited her to join us for breakfast one morning to experience it first hand.

Toward the end of lunch, Marilyn asked about my involvement with *The Vicar of Dibley*. "I noticed in the TV guides that you were the person on whom it was based," she said.

"Oh, not really," I replied. "I was an unofficial, friendly advisor to the show. Richard Curtis, the writer, and Dawn French came to visit me, and a relationship was begun. As you can see, my work in the inner city is a far cry from the green pastures of Dibley."

I tried to downplay my association with the show and return her focus to the real-life work going on in our inner-city churches. I knew that Martin really wanted to talk more with her about the Church Urban Fund, and so did I. Marilyn, however, was undeterred. She wanted to know more about women priests and their ministry and about mine in particular. The first anniversary of the ordination of women to the priesthood was approaching and a new idea was forming in her mind. I think poor Martin began to wish he had never invited me to lunch.

A few days later, Marilyn called me with her idea. "I want to make a documentary about you and your work in the inner city, linking it with *The Vicar of Dibley*. It will be perfect to mark the first anniversary of women priests," she said excitedly.

"What about the Church Urban Fund?" I asked, concerned that Martin's original plan might get lost. "Could we still have a big chunk of the program raising the profile of the Fund?"

"Absolutely," replied Marilyn.

And so the documentary *Not the Vicar of Dibley,* which became part of the BBC's 1995 "Everyman" series, was conceived. The producer and research assistant, Alex and Annie, were two women who had been signed up by Marilyn to make the documentary. They were both warm and supportive, and it was easier than I expected to have them shadow me for two months. They looked through my daily and weekly diary and decided, with some suggestions from me, what they wanted to film. There was lots going on, including a baptism and a wedding, and it was with concern and excitement that I embarked on this rather unusual venture at a busy time of year.

Our first filming attempt was a bit of a disaster. The parish weekend away had been scheduled in February. Lots of families with children from Immanuel Church were going away together to Ashburnham, a beautiful country house conference center in Battle, near Hastings. The film crew's hope was to get some interesting shots of an inner-city congregation having fun together in the beautiful countryside. Kids from the city would be seen running free and breathing fresh air.

The film crew, which consisted of Alex, Annie, a cameraman, and a sound technician, booked into a local hotel and joined us for the weekend. Poised and ready with their camera and boom stick, they waited and waited. It rained all weekend without stopping. In the end, they decided to film anyway and we all took walks in the mud and the rain, looking like drowned rats at the end of the day. They also filmed inside as we ate meals, held church services, and talked together in small groups.

It was the first time any of us had been trailed by a camera crew and it was difficult to get used to. "Just act naturally and pretend we're not here," said Alex. It was easier said than done. "Don't look directly into the camera while we're filming or we won't be able to use that shot," were our instructions. But the camera was hard to ignore when it suddenly loomed two feet from my nose as I was eating a mouthful of cereal or taking a slurp of tea, and it was difficult to be natural when I felt so self-conscious.

In the end, none of the footage from the weekend was used in the final program, but it had not been a waste of time. The congregation had got to know and like the production team, and vice versa. It was good practice having the camera around and, throughout the weeks, that followed, of filming in the church and parish, we all felt much more at ease and viewed the crew as an extension of our already unusual family.

The camera literally followed me around for weeks and I had a microphone hidden under my clerical shirt. Everywhere I went, the crew came with me: including my shopping at Sainsbury's. As I wandered around the aisles with my cart, people nodded and said "Hello," while children nudged their mums, saying, "Look, Mum it's a TV camera." Suddenly a woman stopped me as I was picking up some lemons. She was quite unaware of the camera or that she was being filmed. She patted my arm beaming, "It's so good to see a woman priest. I'm so happy for you. What a fabulous green shirt, I always knew it would take the women to bring a bit of color into the church! You women bring more humanity and are less fossilized. Some of those men are so miserable and uninspiring."

She then went off on a tirade about a local clergyman who had upset her. She got more and more angry and had more and more choice things to say about the clergyman. I made sympathetic noises and said that I hoped she would have a better experience of church now that women were on the scene. As we parted, the cameraman stopped filming and bounded over. "That was great, did you plant her?" She had been so spontaneous and had said such good stuff that he thought I had set her up. Annie, the research assistant, quickly approached the baffled woman and explained that they had just filmed her conversation with me, "Could we have your permission to use it?"

"By all means," said the woman and, after giving Annie her name, walked away looking very pleased to have helped the cause!

The angry words about the clergyman were cut from the final program, but her warm encouragement was used. This was typical of the way Alex and Annie shaped the whole documentary. They weren't looking to make an angry film; they wanted to paint a positive picture of a woman at work as a priest in the church and for it to appear as the most natural thing in the world. They filmed me preaching and dancing (though not at the same time). They filmed me as I bought stamps from the post office and a copy of *The Big Issue* from a homeless street vendor. The camera rolled as I rode my bike around the parish, and they followed me on the subway as I traveled to the General Synod at Westminster.

As I boarded the subway for Westminster, and sat down, the cameraman kept filming from the platform until the doors closed and the train moved away. The man I sat next to asked me, "Were they filming me or you?" It turned out that he was a lord from Ireland on his way to a session at the House of Lords. At the next stop, I got off the train and waited for the crew to arrive on the next one. Then we all boarded the train together to film from the inside of the train. I wonder how many people watching the documentary noticed that the man I sat next to had disappeared!

During filming, I spent hours sitting in my living room or kitchen, talking to the camera, answering questions that Alex asked. Some of this material was woven into the program and some of what I said was used as a voiceover for other scenes. It was emotionally draining for me to sit for so long, thinking and talking. By the time we finished, we had hours and hours of footage of me talking, and just a relatively small amount of it was used in the final film.

Not the Vicar of Dibley was a good title for the documentary: much like *Not the Nine O'clock News,* it communicated exactly what the documentary was and was not about. The final, edited program began with a close-up shot of me putting on lipstick in the vestry, removing my jewelry, and putting on my cassock alb in preparation for a service. My voice was heard speaking in the background.

"The image of someone who was terribly holy and spiritual and had nothing to do with worldly things wasn't me, and I wondered, 'Is it possible to be a normal human being, a young woman working in the church as a priest?

The baptism of Harry and George
Hellis, filmed for the documentary
Not the Vicar of Dibley, showed the
church in a very positive,
welcoming light.

Can I combine my personality, my life, my interest in the world with being a priest?' I decided that the answer to that was yes, I could, and that I would have a go."

An actor's voice then introduced me. "Last year, the walls of a four-hundred-year-old tradition finally fell, as women were ordained into the Anglican priesthood. Prior to their ordination, women had only been accepted in the junior role of deacon. Joy Carroll had worked for six years in that capacity when she caught the eye of writer Richard Curtis, who took her as his model for the main character in the television series *The Vicar of Dibley*. The reality of Joy's working life in her South London parish couldn't be further from the green pastures of Dibley."

In my weeks of being trailed by a camera, the scheduled baptism — for a baby and his older brother from our congregation — had been filmed. The image of that service in the program was a very positive one, with children seen dancing as the adults sang hymns. The church was portrayed as a warm and welcoming place for the whole family. The scene came across particularly well as it was accompanied by some words from Richard Curtis. He and I had become friends, and it had been wonderful to have him as a guest at my ordination to the priesthood.

"I got a bee in my bonnet about women vicars after seeing a friend of mine get married," said Richard on the program. "It suddenly struck me as very odd that in an intimate area of life when so often it's your mother who's more interested in your romances and your children and things like that, how perverse it is that it's so often middle-aged, bachelor men who are in charge of these things that would be much more suited to a woman to do. I then became sure of the fact that women priests were a very good and needed thing in society."

For part of the documentary, Dawn French agreed to meet me at the Groucho Club in London and have our conversation filmed. She talked about some of the feedback she had received from *The Vicar of Dibley*. "I've had a very good response from people who are in the church, mostly female priests, and they really liked it. They've written for fashion advice...where did you get that jumper? Some people have objected to it, but I think we knew from the start that that would be the case."

I added that I was grateful to Dawn for the way she had portrayed the vicar, saying, "My women priest friends love the show. They have told me that it has helped to make them more accessible and approachable to people in general. It was great that she was such a human character."

"Although she was the only one who was," quipped Dawn. "The rest of the people in that village were pretty odd!" I was glad for the opportunity to show through the documentary that not all those who are Christians, or involved in a church, are odd. Indeed, they are often the people who are most actively committed to the most vulnerable in their communities.

My dad was introduced in the documentary with the following words: "Joy's own father was a pioneer in the movement to reinvigorate the role of the church in urban areas." Dad then spoke about my early years and was clearly very proud. "We moved to St. Stephen's Church in South Lambeth. It was a situation where groups of lads would be standing on street corners, threatening anyone to pass by. It really was a difficult area in those days. Joy was brought up in that background. She went to the local school, and there she really survived and showed herself as a leader. There were lots of leaders leading in different directions, and I like to think that Joy and her following were a leadership for good."

Partly because of my upbringing, I have always felt most at home in the inner city. I was glad that the issues facing those living in the city were highlighted in *Not the Vicar of Dibley*. The cameras showed me at a day center for the homeless and spending time in the Beehive Café. In the documentary, I said, "It's really important to believe in the value of every human being, whatever their status. If somebody has had a rough time in life, lost their job, and things have gone from bad to worse for them and they find themselves without a home, that person is still as important and valuable as you or I, and we have a responsibility to respond to them."

One scene of the documentary showed me watching one of my favorite episodes of *The Vicar of Dibley*. The episode reflected some of my own politics, which was very satisfying for me.

"What was that socialist tract you were spouting from the pulpit last Sunday?" asks the local Dibley landowner and councilor.

"I've got a feeling it was the Sermon on the Mount," replies the vicar.

"Jesus did not tell rich people to give all their money away to the poor," he complains.

"I think you'll find that he did, actually," she replies.

Unfortunately, the Church Urban Fund should have been featured more than it was in the final documentary. We spent a whole day at the Church Urban Fund office, filming interviews and talking about the Fund. Those scenes were never used and I felt sorry about that, especially as it was supposed to be a documentary about the Fund in the first place.

Instead, one of the aims of the film was clearly to encourage the acceptance of women priests and to advance their progress in the church vocationally. "Joy works alongside David Isherwood, who is the senior vicar," said the voiceover. "Inequalities are, it seems, still entrenched in the institution, and very few women have yet acquired the singular status of working alone as the vicar of a parish." Technically, this was true. But the reality was that David and I enjoyed a very equal working partnership. I'm not convinced that working alone is altogether desirable for women *or* men. The point being made, however, was that women now could and should be appointed to positions of seniority without delay or discrimination.

I was fortunate to be a priest in a diocese that was very supportive of women. Bishop Roy Williamson has since retired, but he fearlessly supported the women in his diocese and did his best to appoint women priests to significant positions whenever he was able. With a twinkle in his eye and a song in his voice, the Irish bishop was an ideal person to interview for the documentary.

"Some people have a gut reaction about seeing a woman as a priest celebrating the Eucharist or seeing a woman in charge of a parish. They feel it is quite impossible for a woman to exercise headship in this particular way," said Bishop Williamson. "Others feel that, since Christ never ordained a woman or didn't even have a woman as one of his twelve disciples, it isn't right for the church to take this departure. So there's a whole gamut of reasons, and many of them are held sincerely, but I don't agree with any of them." What a good bloke!

I was particularly pleased that the documentary portrayed me as "myself." I love parties: I love going to them and I love having them. I had planned a 1970s bad-taste party at my house, and there are some great scenes of my friends and parishioners looking ridiculous as they danced to hits from the 1970s, with disco lights flashing.

There were also some very funny moments while filming. For example, I was preparing for the Ash Wednesday service at the beginning of Lent and needed to burn last year's palm crosses to make the ashes. I knew that Alex wanted to film this, but I was nervous that I might do something liturgically incorrect in front of millions of viewers. I found a book on liturgy and learned that one is not supposed to set a flame to the palm crosses. The palms must simply incinerate until they turn to ash. I had no idea how to make this happen. After asking lots of colleagues who didn't know either, I decided to heat up the palms in my frying pan until they "incinerated."

There I was in the kitchen, pushing palm crosses around the pan with a wooden spoon, feeling very silly and speaking into the camera, "I'm sure this isn't quite the right way to do this, but we need some incinerated ashes and this is an attempt to make that happen. I'm

In my study at home, as associate vicar of Immanuel, Streatham Common.

sure there's a liturgical way in which one is supposed to do this in a very ceremonious fashion but they seem to be burning up quite nicely."

I felt more and more foolish as the demonstration went on and began to laugh, "This is rather like *The Vicar of Dibley* isn't it? This is the sort of thing Dawn French would be doing in the series, panicking about how to burn the palm crosses on Ash Wednesday. Oh, dear, I'll probably get lots of phone calls from very experienced priests telling me how I've done this so wrong. Oh, well, you live and learn!"

In fact, no one did call to criticize my method, just to say what a good idea it was. What they didn't know was that my house was filled with smoke for days afterwards!

Ash Wednesday was a very special service for me as this was my first as a priest. "God, our Father, you create us from the dust of the earth. Grant that these ashes may be for us a sign of our penitence and a symbol of our mortality, for it is by your grace alone that we receive eternal life in Jesus Christ our Savior, Amen." David and I marked each other with the ashes, and then made a cross on the forehead of each member of the congregation with the words, "Remember that you are dust, and to dust you shall return. Turn away from sin and be faithful to Christ."

The last scenes in *Not the Vicar of Dibley* are from a wedding that I conducted. The couple that got married were wonderfully original and unorthodox, and I think we presented an image of a church that could be relevant to today's generation. The bride wore a beautiful green gown, and the groom a tartan suit. It happened to be April Fools' Day, which explained why the best man was dressed as a jester. There was, nevertheless, a sense of serious commitment and celebration in the air; it was the perfect note on which to end the film. As I was shown leading the marriage service, Richard Curtis was heard saying, "I felt sure that the moment people saw a woman in a dog collar, in action, it would immediately make sense to them." It's true that the more people actually experience the ministry of women, the more comfortable and accepting of it they become. I hoped that this program might be another way for more people to have a positive experience of women's ministry.

It wasn't just a positive image of women priests that I wanted to portray. The documentary was a wonderful opportunity for me to present a positive image of the church, and therefore of God, to the general public. It came at a time when the church was besieged with scandal caused by badly behaved vicars. In the eyes of the world, it appeared to be in a sorry state. The church is by no means perfect and has been the cause of much misery for a lot of people, but I consider it worth building up. In the film I put it this way: "There is a difference between the institution of the church, which I find quite difficult at times, and God. I stay within the institution because I believe in a God who isn't bound by it."

Chapter Eleven

The Great Banquet of Life

It has always been important to me to safeguard my sense of self. I have seen too many clergy have their identity consumed by their role. Time off and recreation have always been essential to my self-preservation. If I go on vacation or go out socially and meet new people, I'm usually quite grateful if people don't introduce me as a priest before we've had time to get to know each other a bit: it can be a real conversation killer! People aren't always interested in getting to know a priest. They have an image of what they think a priest is or should be like, which they immediately attach to you.

I love *The Vicar of Dibley* episode when Geraldine has a crush on Tristan, the producer of *Songs of Praise*, precisely because it highlights the vulnerability of the character, reminding us that even clergy are human. It was a scene from this episode that gave me the idea for the title of the British edition of this book.

"You'll be keeping the sermon in then will you?" Geraldine calls from the kitchen.

"Oh, yes. It's very much the heart of the program. I'd really love people to get a glimpse of the woman underneath the cassock," replies Tristan.

"I assume you're talking spiritually there," quips Geraldine. "Yes, I'm talking spiritually."

Geraldine then chastises herself in the kitchen. "What else could he have meant — 'I want to get a close up of your pants'?"

My support network of family and friends that existed before I went to theological college became more important than ever once I started work as a minister. I made it a priority to spend time with them. In the inner city, where life and work are inextricably entwined and where parishioners need a great deal more than the usual level of clerical support, I could easily have become engulfed by the job. The concerts, films, and parties, the London social life outside the parish, which I had been afraid I might lose when I went to theological college, now became my lifeline.

I had grown up knowing a large number of clerical families, and I'd seen enough of vicarage life to know that I didn't want to be destroyed by it. Too many clergy ruin their marriages, neglect their kids, or drink themselves to death because they lose their sense of perspective; their self-identity is swallowed up by the role. I jealously guarded my own time. I took time off regularly to be with family and friends, especially nurturing my friendships outside the church. I took in lodgers and worked out at the local gym, where I valued not having to talk to anyone. My personal tutor at Cranmer Hall had written on my final report, "Joy will never be prone to becoming a workaholic." At the time I had been unsettled by the comment. Did he think I was lazy? Now I am glad for his astute observation and thankful that he was right.

I had a number of lifelines when it came to my private life, one of which was the support I got from my parents. Dad retired in 1994, the same year that I was ordained a priest. He and mum moved out of the vicarage in Purley and moved to a smaller house they had bought in Old Coulsdon. It was a great support to have them so nearby. It was easy to jump in the car and visit them for lunch or an evening meal. Their wisdom and years of experience were a rich pool for me to draw from, and they always understood the frustrations of being a minister. When Dad still worked, I was always known as John Carroll's daughter, and it was a source of amusement and pride for him that people now said, "Oh, you must be Joy Carroll's father."

My other lifelines came in the form of some very important friends, and two in particular nourished my soul. Keith was someone I had known since I'd been at teacher-training college in Plymouth. On weekends, he often came to stay on campus with our barman, Johnny. Every Sunday night, Johnny's country-and-western band played in a local pub, and a group of us often went to the gig. Keith was from California but lived in South London, and I once heard it said that he was the best banjo player in the country. We became friends over the course of his visits and continued to be friends back in South London when college was over.

I loved to listen to Keith's music and meet his friends. One winter I even took my skiing vacation in Interlaken, Switzerland, where he and his friend were working for the season. That vacation I listened to country music by night and skied with Keith by day. In a way, Keith represented a complete escape from my church world, and I found it refreshing and challenging to see the world through the eyes of an agnostic.

Father Cunningham, or Marnie, was an Irish Catholic parish priest in Manchester and another good friend. Marnie had been the director of pastoral theology and the vice principal at Ushaw Seminary in Durham. We'd become friends while I was living at the seminary on the exchange program. Marnie had been a rugby player before he became a priest. His strong, rugged frame and warm, weathered face were as much a part of him as his lively and rooted spirituality. Marnie was 100 percent in support of my calling to priesthood and remained a wonderful friend after I left Durham.

About three times a year, Marnie would have cause to visit London, and I would get a call. "Joy, I'm going to be in town for a few days — can we meet up? There's a film I want to see and perhaps we could see a play, too?" Whenever I heard that warm, Irish voice I knew I would be clearing the time in my diary somehow. We would spend the whole day in the West End and would often see two films or plays and then talk long and hard over a Chinese meal in Soho. Sadly, Marnie is gone now: he lost a long and well-fought battle with leukemia and died in the year 2000.

I had one particular group of friends who had been at theological college with me and who were also priests in South London's Southwark Diocese. We played bridge together at college and loved to cram in a game whenever four busy clergy diaries could find a couple of hours free at the same time. As we all got busier, it became more and more difficult to make it work. In desperation one night we organized an all-night bridge game in Clapham, where one of the bridge players was a curate. The four of us were to gather there as soon as we could once our evening meetings were finished.

"The grace of our Lord Jesus Christ, the love of God and the fellowship of the Holy Spirit be with us all ever-more. Amen." The Parish Church Council meeting was over. I looked at my watch. "I could be on the road by 10:30 p.m. if I get away quickly," I thought. I wondered what the faithful folks gathered around the table would think if they knew I was off to play cards all night! I jumped into my car and set off for Clapham, looking forward to a long, uninterrupted night of bridge.

Suddenly I heard the screech of tires ahead of me. Someone about four cars ahead had stopped unexpect-edly — perhaps a cat had run into the road. In any case, the cars each began to run into the one in front with a loud crash each time. I braked for what seemed like an eternity and finally stopped just a fraction of an inch short of col-lision. "I made it," I thought. Then another car ploughed into the back of mine, pushing me into the one in front. There I was, car number four in a five-car pile up. I tried to get out, but the doors wouldn't open. I was shaken and jolted but unharmed, and I just waited to be rescued. When I was finally freed from the wreckage, I stepped into the kebab shop and called my friends. By the time they arrived to get me, I had made my statements to the police, seen my totaled car towed away, and was ready to play.

After that eventful night, we decided to work on other ways to find "bridge time" and so our annual bridge vaca-tions were born. Usually in the autumn, eight of us would rent a house on the Isle of Wight, or a cottage in Wales, for six days. We played bridge every day, had bracing walks along the beach, took it in turns to cook fabu-lous meals, and were all home in time for our respective churches on Sunday. It was a mixed group of married couples and single people, and it was on those vacations that I had time to think about the fact that I wasn't married. Generally speaking, I was happy not to be married.

A bit of a cynic, I was realistic about the unsatisfactory marriages of many of my friends and never wished myself in their shoes. Having said that, there were times when I longed for the security of a special partner in life. My ideal man would love independence in a relationship, not be too needy, love me in spite of my weaknesses, and be there to share life's ups and downs. This was pretty idealistic and, on reflection, just a tad selfish!

Being single had its advantages when it came to being a minister, especially in the inner city. I had no ties and no responsibility to another person on a day-to-day basis. I was the only person I had to consider when making plans for time off and vacations, and I could do whatever I chose to in my free time. If I wanted to meet a friend for a drink, see a movie, or watch *Eastenders,* no one else had to approve or agree with my decisions. I could work late at night and visit parishioners whenever it suited them and me. I was single-minded when it came to my work, and no one else was affected.

My relationships never led to marriage usually because I wasn't prepared or able to get to that level of commitment. I went out with some wonderful men and loved being in love. At some point, though, usually after a few months or when the man began to get serious, the spark would disappear, the feeling would leave me, and it would all be over. I hurt people but couldn't seem to break out of the pattern. Each time I began a new relationship, I believed he could be "the one" until the same thing happened again. One of my victims once said to me, "The

trouble with you, Joy, is that you treat men like most
men treat women." Sadly it was true, but I was surprised
by the trace of pleasure I felt when he said it.

One of my relationships had a very different dynamic.
You might say it was payback time. Martin managed a
drop-in center for the homeless. He also helped to run
the CRISIS shelter at Christmas time. I first met him when
he came to check out St. Michael's as the alternative site
for the women. He arrived while the nursery was in session. He was tall, good looking, in great shape, and had a
lovely voice. Setting down his rucksack, he began a very
animated talk with the nursery kids. His charm immediately won their hearts; mine was soon to follow. We had
fun and shared the same values, but there was one important thing we did not share and that was faith in Jesus
Christ. I thought we could make it work but, two years
later, he was the one who couldn't make a commitment
to me. It was my first heartbreak. Now I knew what it
felt like.

In the year that followed I made some bad decisions
that felt even worse because I was an ordained minister
who should have known better. After a whirlwind ro-
mance on a summer vacation with a group of friends,
I agreed to marry Mark, who I had known vaguely for
many years. I didn't realize it at the time, but I still had
not recovered from the break-up with Martin and ended
up breaking off the engagement to Mark. It was probably
the most emotionally painful period of time I can remember. I decided then that I was going to be good to myself,
as well as the rest of the human race, and have no more
relationships — ever. Looking back, I realize that neither
Martin nor Mark, nor any of the other men I fell in love
with were men I could have successfully married. It was

the grace of God that led me to the man who had all the right qualities to partner me through life.

It was Pentecost, June 3, 1995. Streatham Common was one of hundreds of locations across London holding an event called "The Great Banquet," and I was coordinating the Streatham project. The idea was to reenact the Parable of the Great Banquet found in the Gospel of Luke. Churches and faith-based communities around the city would put on a meal or a party, reaching out and serving the people of their respective communities.

The mother of all the banquets was held at Whitehall in the banqueting suite. There, politicians, celebrities, and church leaders ate with post office workers, street cleaners, and folk who worked with the homeless. The idea was to give credence and pride of place to those who were often overlooked out there on the highways and byways. Cardinal Hume served the drinks as people arrived, and the lowliest of guests were given a place of honor. The dinner tables were made up of people from many different backgrounds and walks of life. The centerpiece on each table was a tall vase of water that contained two little goldfish swimming around. After dinner, there was a disco in the undercroft of the banqueting suite, with "Kid" Jensen as the DJ. Those of us who had been organizing local banquets were given tickets to join the party at the end of the day, and it was just what we needed.

In Streatham, our banquet was a picnic on the common. We mobilized area churches to make thousands of sandwiches to give away, and we also had a fête. The Beehive Café became a complimentary Caribbean restaurant for the day, and we had side stalls, music, face painting, games, and a bouncy castle. The whole affair had great potential and was actually a lot of fun, but it poured rain for the whole day, which was very disappointing.

"Come on girls," I said to Jessica, Theresa, and the team of wonderful women who had helped pull the event off. "Let's go and have ourselves some fun!" We'd booked the youth club minibus and I knew that David, the vicar, really wanted to come with us. "Now, David, this is a girls' night out," I said. "You can have a ticket only if you will be our driver." I'm sure he thoroughly enjoyed being the chauffeur to ten rather raucous women set on having a good night out.

There were two guests at the Great Banquet who were visiting from America. One was the Reverend Jesse Jackson and the other was Jim Wallis, the editor of *Sojourners* magazine and a speaker and author. He was on a book tour. I had met Jim a year earlier at the annual Greenbelt Christian arts festival. Amid the program of rock bands and artists, we had sat on a panel together, discussing the question, "What's the point of being an evangelical?" It was good to meet up with him again at the banquet disco, and when he asked if I was going to be able to get to any of his speaking venues, I made a mental note to make the effort. He was speaking in Cambridge ten days later and I could combine that with a visit to my friend Anne, who was the chaplain at Trinity College.

The disco was a great success, and when it was over, we wearily walked back to the minibus. Tracey and I had each taken a vase of goldfish and were carefully trying not to slop them all over the streets of London. I named my fish "Wallace" and "Gromit."

It had been a great evening.

MY APPOINTMENT DIARY at Immanuel was usually booked solid. The week ahead was no different, with a number of funerals, a sermon to prepare, a confirmation rehearsal, visits to people who wanted their babies baptized, a parochial church council meeting, a school assembly, and, on Saturday, a day trip to Brighton with the Parent and Toddler group, where I would be driving the minibus.

I loved my work — even the funerals. As the priest, I was invited into the heart of a bereaved family when they were at their most vulnerable. In funeral visits, I felt very close, very quickly, to people I had never met before. As I listened to them tell me about their loved one who had died and looked at their photographs, I would be able to gain a sense of who the person was, as well as a sense of the people who would miss them. At the service, I always gave a short sermon and eulogy that gave thanks to God for the life that had been lost. The service, with its formal structure and the drama of cremation or burial, was itself a rite of passage that helped people to move on through the grieving process and say goodbye.

I must have performed a thousand funerals, most of them for old folks who had lived a good, long life. The one I was to do that week was no exception: a working-class lady in her nineties who had been through hard times and lived through the war. She had been living in a home for the elderly in Streatham when she died.

There were other funerals that were extremely difficult to do. A young, gay man had been coming to talk with me for about six months on a regular basis, trying to make sense of his strong faith in God, his broken relationship, and the fact that he was living with AIDS. When he was too tired or not feeling well, I would go to his flat. One weekend he was admitted to the hospital with a chest

infection as he had been several times before. I visited
him on Saturday and expected him to be home in a few
days. I was devastated to get a call on Monday from his
friend to say that he had died but was thankful that he
had been able to avoid a lingering and difficult death.

Even though the young man hadn't expected to die so
soon, he had planned his funeral service with me. It was
actually a glorious affair. He had given me a CD with
his favorite versions of the *Magnificat* ("My soul doth
magnify the Lord") and the *Nunc Dimittis* ("Lord, now
you let your servant depart in peace"). It was wonderful
and appropriate that he chose to have the *Nunc Dimittis*
played as his coffin was carried into the chapel and the
Magnificat at the end of the service, when it would usually
be the other way around.

My role as the priest at a funeral is to be the pro-
fessional who facilitates the grieving of others. When I
conducted that funeral, I had to work very hard to keep
my own emotions in check. When I had spoken the last
words and we all sat to listen to the Magnificat, the tears
rolled unashamedly down my face. Other occasions when
I had to fight for control over my emotions were when I
had to do the funerals for babies.

IT WAS WEDNESDAY. Jim Wallis was on his book tour in
Cambridge that night, speaking on *The Soul of Politics*.
Just before the rush hour, I jumped into my car with an
overnight bag and drove to Anne's house in the middle of
Cambridge. She and I went to the event together.

"Hope is believing, in spite of the evidence, and then
watching the evidence change," said Jim as he finished his
talk. He had been talking about his experiences in South
Africa.

Applause erupted around the room and people scuttled off to the table at the back to have Jim sign their books. "That has really inspired me afresh," I said to Anne. Eight years before, my friends at theological college had gone to hear Jim Wallis speak in Newcastle. I hadn't gone and so had never heard him speak before. I was impressed. He said the kinds of things I believed deep inside but had never heard articulated so well. "It's the encouragement we need sometimes to keep doing the work that we're doing," said Anne.

Later on, Jim invited Anne and me to join him and a small group of friends for refreshments at a local watering hole. I was surprised at how pleased I was by the invite. He was strong, gentle, good-looking, had wonderful eyes and a very sexy voice. I wanted to find out more about him personally. For a start, I had no idea whether he was married or not.

I found myself sitting next to him. "That was a great talk, Jim. Thank you." I didn't add that I thought he looked really tired and as though he needed someone to take care of him. His friends almost choked on their drinks when I said, "Well, Jim, are you married?" Anne thought it was an extremely forward thing to ask and told me so later in no uncertain terms.

As we walked home, I asked Jim how much longer he was in England. It was only a few more days, so we arranged to meet for a drink the next day. The following morning, I drove into the city of London. We walked into a pub close by the hotel where Jim was staying and to my surprise, the landlord greeted me like an old friend: "Reverend Carroll. Welcome! How nice to see you." It was an amazing coincidence, but it was his mother I had buried the week before in Streatham. "Your drinks are on the house, Reverend. You did my mother proud." Jim was duly impressed. We sat down and talked like there was no tomorrow.

It was another coincidence that Jim was going to a dinner party that evening with someone I knew well and, since we had a lot more talking to do, we decided that it would be all right if I gate-crashed the party. We jumped in a taxi and left my car parked outside his hotel. No one seemed too disconcerted by my arrival with Jim, though there were a few raised eyebrows. It was fun. One of our mutual friends said to him, "Jim, have you seen the BBC documentary about Joy that was broadcast at Easter? It was very good."

"No, I haven't," said Jim looking interested.

"I have a copy. Why don't we watch it tonight?" said our host, heading for the VCR.

"No way!" I exclaimed. I couldn't imagine anything more embarrassing than having to sit there while everyone watched the show. I insisted that they not watch it, especially as I had gate-crashed their party, so our friend lent Jim the tape to watch back in his hotel room.

When the party was over, we returned to the hotel for me to pick up my car. Jim was leaving the next day for Germany, where he would be on a speaking tour for ten days.

"Well, Jim," I said, "it's been great to catch up with you and have the chance to get to know you a little better. Let's keep in touch." I turned to get in my car.

Jim touched my arm and said, "Why not come in for a nightcap, and we can talk some more." I hesitated. I had to get up early the next morning to pick up Stephen, my eighteen-month-old nephew who I looked after one morning a week, and I still had a thirty-minute drive home. It would have been sensible to decline the invitation, and I almost did. Suddenly I had a feeling that this was one of those seize-the-day moments. Jim was the most interesting person I had talked to for a long time. Here was a once-in-a-lifetime opportunity to spend time with him. I took a deep breath, "Okay, that would be great." That decision changed the course of my life.

There was no bar inside the hotel, but the night porter on duty liked Jim and showed us to a beautiful wood-paneled room with a fireplace and comfortable chairs. A moment later, he appeared with a bottle of wine and glasses. We talked until three o'clock in the morning. This time we talked about ourselves, our strengths and weaknesses, our joys and our sadness, even our relationships. We found that, as well as respecting each other, we liked each other too.

"Isn't it sad that we've just met, we seem to have so much in common, and now you are leaving?" I commented.

"Oh, well, that's life," I thought to myself. As I left, we gave each other a light peck on the cheek and a hug. I assumed that I wouldn't see him again for a year or so. I drove home with a grateful heart — grateful that I had spent such quality time with such a wonderful person. And that was that.

I was bleary-eyed the next morning when I went to pick up Stephen and took him to Morning Prayer with me at church. Stephen's day with me was also the day when other clergy in the area would join me, and it was fun to see their relationship with him get warmer as they got used to having a little one in their midst. Stephen was always very well behaved during the short service. He sat in his stroller drinking milk and eating a snack. It was especially amusing when he went through a phase of needing to hold a pair of his mum's silky panties close to his face while he sucked his thumb. As soon as prayers were over, we went into the Beehive Café for our breakfast. Stephen loved to eat the "big breakfast," of sausages, eggs, and beans, and would delight the customers with his sweet smiles and giggles.

When we finally got back to my house, there was a message on my answering machine from Jim Wallis. "Joy, I just watched your video this morning and I wanted to let you know that I thought it was great. It gave a very positive picture of the church. I wondered if there was any chance that you might be able to meet me for lunch at the airport before I fly to Germany?"

I looked at my diary. I could just about do it. "Great!" I thought to myself with a surprising feeling of excitement in my stomach.

At the airport, we found a place to sit and chat. As we talked, the chemistry between us was clear and our hands touched across the table. That was it; we knew we had made a romantic connection. All of a sudden, fire alarms started ringing all around us and we could hardly hear each other. "Come on," I said. "Let's get out of here and go for a walk."

I took Jim's hand. "Where are we going to walk at Heathrow Airport . . . along the runway?" Jim was unsure where we could go. Soon we were outside the building. I looked around desperately for somewhere to sit and talk.

"Over there," I said pointing to the luggage carts. There was a ledge behind them that we could sit on. Very soon, we were kissing passionately behind those luggage carts. Every now and then, someone would come to get a cart and find us there. "Oh, I'm so sorry, excuse me," they would say, probably wondering why two mature people were down there, making out like teenagers. Fortunately, no one knew that it was the international author and speaker Jim Wallis and "the real vicar of Dibley" that they had stumbled across!

As we waited for Jim's flight, he tried to persuade me to take a vacation and visit him in August. Everything had happened so suddenly that I needed to think about it. When I said, "Don't you think that would be a rather reckless thing to do?" He replied, "Don't you have a theology of recklessness?" Thus began a two-year, transatlantic relationship. One of Jim's friends later called it a "GIR," a Geographically Impossible Relationship.

Jim did indeed manage to persuade me to visit him in August, when we spent a few days on Block Island and then a few more in New York City. One night on the beautiful, unspoiled island, we stood on the cliffs watching a dramatic thunderstorm rage over the ocean. I turned to Jim and asked, "Well, we've had some wonderful days together. Is that all this can be? Where do we go from here? What exactly am I to you?"

He looked at me with a smile and said, "In America we'd say that you're my 'main squeeze.' "

I dropped his hand and looked at him. "What a horrible phrase," I thought to myself.

"Now listen," I said firmly, "if our relationship is to go any further, I need to be your only squeeze."

Once that was settled, we agreed to give it a try. We both had worthwhile and satisfying vocations and a future together was uncertain. We knew it would be complicated from the start. For two years we found creative ways to be with each other, and it was a very exciting time.

We began by discovering each other's worlds — of home and work. In October, I made a short trip to

Washington, D.C., for just four days. In November, Jim
came to London for a week. In that week, he watched
the whole series of *The Vicar of Dibley* in one sitting. I
introduced him to Indian takeout, and we went to the
theater. Jim even came to one of our church social events
in a local pub — a darts tournament. Jim paired up with
Arthur, the headmaster of our church school, and gave
everyone a great laugh with his throwing style. He had
never thrown a dart before and looked very much like
he was throwing a javelin. To everyone's surprise Arthur
and Jim won and Jim even threw the winning shot. My
brother presented him with his winner's pint and said,
"You Americans! You come over here, steal our women,
drink our beer, and beat us at our own games!"

After spending Christmas with my family, Jim took a
bookwriting month away from the *Sojourners* magazine
office. England seemed like a good place to write. In fact,
whenever Jim was invited to speak in England, he now accepted. During our two-year courtship, we even managed
to take vacations on each side of the Atlantic. One was in
Acapulco, Mexico, and the other in the Greek Islands. It
was almost too romantic.

"Jim, I need a dose of reality to see if this is going to
work. We need to spend a chunk of time living and dating
in the same city," I said. I began to explore how I might
arrange an exchange with an American priest. A couple of
weeks later, I was sitting in one of the conference rooms of
Church House in Westminster with my women colleagues
of the General Synod. At the end of the meeting, one of
them had an announcement to make.

"I have received a letter from the College of Preachers
in Washington, D.C." My ears pricked up at the mention
of Washington. "We have been asked to send a couple of

representatives to attend a conference on 'Women's Leadership in the Anglican Communion.' " Would anyone here be interested in going? Let me know afterwards."

I was quick to volunteer. My motivation for attending the conference wasn't entirely altruistic, of course: it was a great opportunity to visit Jim. As it turned out, the conference was excellent and I made some important connections with diocesan clergy and laity that were to be extremely helpful in my quest to spend time in Washington.

One morning during the conference, I had coffee with David, the rector of Grace Church in Washington's Georgetown neighborhood. He was English. Not only did he speak my language, he understood the Church of England that I came from and was happy to help. "Joy, I have been planning to take a three-month sabbatical next year. Perhaps you might be able to cover for me here at Grace," he said. I immediately began to work on making that possibility a reality.

My bishop and parish were harder to convince, but I was eventually able to persuade Bishop Martin and my church to allow me to take a short sabbatical. I was eager to have their approval, but they knew that if they didn't give it, I might resign anyway. I was glad not to have to do that.

Grace Church in Washington gave me a job, a place to live, and a car to drive. Finally, Jim and I could figure out whether or not this was going to be forever. Preaching every week in an American church was a new challenge. I prepared diligently to meet the needs of a very different kind of congregation. Most of the members were university educated professionals and looked for intellectual stimulus as well as inspiration from the sermons they heard.

One Sunday I prepared a message especially for the children. I took a can of dog food to church. Once I had everyone's attention, I opened it with a can opener and spooned out the contents into a bowl. I had gathered the children at the front of the church and I held up the can for them to see.

"What is this?" I asked.

"Dog food!" they yelled.

"You're right," I said and put a great big spoonful in my mouth. Everyone in the church gasped with horror. They didn't know that I had previously emptied out the dog food and replaced it with a mixture of a chopped-up "Mars bar" and chocolate instant whip.

"Mmm, this is delicious," I exclaimed as they grimaced and groaned. "Would you like to try some?" I held out the spoon to the children.

The whole church was squirming now and I could see that some of the adults were thinking, "What is she doing?"

"Oh, what? You've never tried this? You mean Americans don't eat dog food?" I asked with amazement.

I hammed it up until one brave kid decided to have a taste. It was a great moment when he realized that it tasted really good and joined me in trying to persuade the others to try it. My dog food trick was illustrating that you can't always tell what's on the inside by looking at the outside, as God will surprise you. There's a verse in the book of Isaiah that says, "Taste and see how good the Lord is." The church never forgot the crazy English woman who pretended to eat dog food.

Jim and I had agreed that, at the end of my stay in Washington, we would decide whether or not to get married. It was difficult. Both of us would have preferred more time, but this was all we had. I had no desire to go back to the transatlantic relationship with no clarity about the future: it was now or never.

We planned to spend a week on Block Island once the Easter services were over. It would either mark the end or the beginning for us as a couple. We sat on the sand dunes beside the lighthouse as the sun set. I was crazy about this man. I had never had such respect for a partner. He was wise, passionate, and prophetic, as well as incredibly attractive, warm, and loving. I was ready, but right up until that evening I wasn't 100 percent sure whether Jim was able to make a definite commitment to marriage. He had done it once before and it had failed miserably. I had been careful not to pressure him. My heart was in my mouth.

As the blazing ball of fire plunged down behind the horizon, Jim said, "Well, shall we do this thing then?"

"What thing?" I asked. I wanted him to be sure and verbalize exactly what he meant.

"This marriage thing." He had said it; the "M" word. From that moment on, despite the bumbling proposal, he never looked back.

Chapter Twelve

Leaving

In June 1997, the whole of Southwark Diocese — both clergy and laity — were encouraged to attend a day out together at Ardingly Show Ground in Surrey. Buses delivered thousands of people to gather for a day of fun and fellowship. My bishop, Roy Williamson, had asked Jim to speak at the event alongside the archbishop of Canterbury, George Carey.

I was in my element: friends and colleagues from the diocese and from both of the churches I had worked in were all around; my family were there with their churches, and my future husband was to address the gathering. I felt very proud. At the same time I felt a twinge of sadness that marrying Jim would mean losing my close involvement with many of these wonderful people. I had handed in my resignation with a heavy heart.

Sometimes the choices we make in life don't feel like choices at all. I knew that marrying Jim was the right thing for me. I was completely in love, and it was my heart's greatest desire. A new and exciting world was about to unfold before me, but I was to do a lot of grieving for the things and people I was leaving behind. When Bishop Roy announced our engagement at the event, I felt a rush of joyful anticipation and I prayed hard for the strength it would take to leave my world.

Leaving Britain to live in America was one of the hardest things I would ever have to do, and my farewell service at Immanuel was extremely moving. I was very happy to see that Keith Hill, our local Labor MP, was sitting in the congregation, as we had met and worked together on several occasions. As I spoke to the congregation for the last time, one of the things I said was, "Hard as it is to leave, there is one thing that has made it just a little easier. Now that we finally have a Labor government, I can at least go knowing that the country is, at last, in good hands." Keith smiled — we were all still in the heady aftermath days of the landslide 1997 election victory that Labor had achieved.

There were a few things I really wanted to do and see before I left the country, and I wanted Jim to experience more of Britain with me before we left it for good. We talked almost every day on the telephone and would have done well to own shares in one or two phone companies. We had a wedding to plan and, before that, Jim was coming to visit for three weeks in August. It would be the last time we would see each other before the wedding in October.

One evening in particular, I was stretched out on the couch after a long day. It was 10:00 p.m., and I waited for Jim to answer the phone. Since Washington is five hours behind, he would just be finishing up at the office. We talked about the contents of our days, and then I floated my idea past him.

"How about we do a farewell tour of Britain, visiting the places in my life that have been significant or special to me?" I ventured. "In each place I could share some of my memories and the experiences I had there. Then I could begin my future with you, happy in the knowledge that you understand some of my past, and I will have said goodbye."

"That sounds good to me," Jim replied, "but could we include a trip to Paris? I've always wanted to go there."

"It's a deal."

We did a lot of driving that summer. Starting in Devon, we visited my old friend from theological college, Susie, and her family. Then we went to look around my old college, St. Mark and St. John's just outside Plymouth. We even found the beach at Mothecombe where I used to take the kids on Pathfinder camp.

From there we made our way to Wales and the beautiful Llanthony Abbey, where we languished for several days and rode horses across the hills. I have always loved Wales, and it's the country where Jim proudly has his ancestral roots. In one remote village, we found the Celtic bands that would be our wedding rings.

In Durham we stayed in rooms at my old college. It was a delight to show off such a wonderful English city to Jim. The memories came flooding back. "This is the boat house where we kept our boat when I rowed with the Cranmer women. . . . This is where I lived with Susie and Katie. . . . This was my favorite walk beside the River Wear." There was a lamp that I particularly loved that was underneath one of the bridges. I called it the "Narnia lamp" from *The Lion, the Witch and the Wardrobe*. And so we talked about our love of C. S. Lewis and his writing.

A seven-hour drive took us back to London before leaving the next morning for a weekend in Paris. We took the Eurostar train through the Channel Tunnel in just three hours and spent the next two days drinking in the essence of that romantic city. We explored remote, cobbled back streets that wound up and down hills. We stumbled across town squares full of artists selling their wares and offering to draw flattering portraits. We sat in gorgeous old churches that invoked the presence of God. We happily rode the train home, but little did we know that, in less that twenty-four hours, Paris would be the scene of a historic tragedy.

It had been a very active vacation and I was exhausted when I collapsed into my bed late on Sunday night. A few hours before, we had been in Paris. I was used to waking up to the mellow sounds of Radio 4 and sometimes the words mingled with strange dreams as I moved into wakefulness. I couldn't believe my ears and thought I was still dreaming when I heard that Princess Diana had been killed in a car accident in Paris. I burst into tears. Surprisingly, I felt as though a friend had just died. I cried as I told Jim what had happened, which left him a little bemused. "I didn't know you were a royalist," he said. "I'm not," I replied with a sniff.

Throughout the day, we listened to the story unfold, as did the rest of the nation, and indeed the world. In the days that followed, an extraordinary grief gripped the country. Jim returned to the United States with a story for his next column. We will both always remember where we were when Princess Diana died.

On the day of Diana's funeral, tearful crowds lined the streets of the funeral procession route and surrounded Westminster Abbey. It was a farewell that anyone who was there will never forget. I planned to be at home, watching the coverage on TV, but my sister-in-law, Julie, decided that she wanted to go and be with the crowds. She wanted to be a part of the historic and moving event.

Going to the funeral meant going to the Abbey the night before and sleeping on the pavement. Julie begged me to go with her. A night sleeping on a hard pavement didn't appeal to me at all, but eventually she persuaded me. We packed up our sleeping bags and supplies for the night and traveled to Westminster on the subway. There were already huge numbers of people gathered; some had been there for several days. We found our spot at the foot of Big Ben and laid down our blanket. Any available space was quickly claimed. Before long we were surrounded by all kinds of people who had joined the crowd for all kinds of reasons.

On one side of us was a family of working-class women spanning three generations. The old mum sat on a fold-up chair and chain-smoked her way through the night. Her three daughters and their children were all around her with candles and pictures of Diana. On the other side of us was what appeared to be a very well-to-do couple, not at all used to sleeping out. Black and white, rich and poor were there in a crowd that was fairly representative of British society.

As the hours passed, the spaces available on the pavement quickly disappeared and people began safeguarding their territory vehemently. One young man appeared beside us and simply stood in silence for a long time. He had cropped red hair and wore a black suit. He had nothing with him. No blanket, no bag, no nothing. We felt a bit sorry for him and eventually we persuaded him to join us. He was a social worker from Manchester called Vic.

As the night wore on, we got to know the people in the pavement space around us. We talked, laughed, and cried together and soon formed quite a bond with these people we had only just met. I decided to put off telling them that I was a priest for as long as possible, as I worried that people might not feel able to be themselves with a priest in the group.

Barriers had been erected alongside the road and even the police on crowd control duty were becoming friendly faces. There were two priests who had been assigned by Westminster Abbey to offer pastoral care to the crowd. They walked up and down the road, greeting and talking to people. As they passed by our patch of pavement, I realized that one of them was a friend of mine. He saw me sitting with our group and called out in rather a loud voice, "Hey, Joy Carroll! I might have known you would be the priest on the other side of the barriers, sleeping out with everyone else." He had blown my cover completely.

"So you're a priest," someone said. A woman priest was still a novelty, and our little camp was intrigued. Instead of making anyone feel uncomfortable, the fact that I was a priest actually seemed to give permission for people to talk about deeper things. We had the rest of the night and covered a lot of ground. Vic, an agnostic, was particularly full of questions. We all talked about life, death, the spiritual journey and finding God, and, in particular relation to Diana, the search for integrity and healing.

Many people felt connected to Diana, especially in her search for wholeness. She had begun to find meaning in her life as she reached out and gave of herself to others. Perhaps as she began to speak up for the people Jesus called "the least of these" she was being spiritually awakened. Whatever her journey, it was tragically and abruptly ended on the roller coaster of a celebrity lifestyle.

The funeral service, relayed via loud speakers, was incredibly moving. You could have heard a pin drop as the procession passed by. On top of the coffin was a simple arrangement of white flowers. The card attached read, "Mummy." It was a night and a day I would never forget.

Almost two years later, in America, I opened an e-mail that read, "Sorry to bother you. I'm searching for a Joy Carroll, who I met at the funeral of Princess Diana. Joy was a vicar at Streatham, I believe, and was off to America to be married. Any info will be appreciated."

I responded to the sender, to let him know that I was indeed the person he was looking for and he replied, "Joy! Wow! I knew I would find you. It's me. The geezer from Manchester. The rebel without a clue." Vic, the agnostic social worker had become a bit of a Web master and had tracked me down via the Net. "The real reason I contacted you," he said, "was to thank you for inspiring me to move forward in my search to find Jesus. Anyway, I found the guy and believe God is on my side and everything looks rosy. Life seems easier to cope with when you can pray to God and He answers. I don't want to get too deep but meeting you was a very important part of my spiritual future. So thanks, mate! I'm not a member of any church as yet, no one will have me!"

That same month, I preached a sermon in Washington on the story of Saint Philip's encounter with the Ethiopian eunuch on the road to Gaza, from Acts, chapter 8. I told my story of Vic because, like Philip, without any planning or orchestration, it seems I was in the right place at the right time to be of some help on the day of Princess Diana's funeral.

IT WAS FINALLY OCTOBER. The newsstands of South London displayed a poster that read "The Vicar of Dibley Marries." Our impending wedding was causing a lot of excitement, especially for the Dibley fans in the congregation. They had heard the rumor that Dawn French and her comedian husband, Lenny Henry, would be among the guests.

Dawn didn't let them down. People craned their necks to get a glimpse of the famous pair and were not disappointed. She arrived with Lenny, wearing a beautiful, large hat, reminding us as she does that "big is beautiful." It wasn't at all out of place as I had chosen a big, traditional dress, made of green velvet and ivory silk. Our guests packed into the Church of Immanuel.

My father stood at the front of the church waiting to marry his daughter. As the organ played, the wedding party processed down the aisle in pairs, mothers and bridesmaids escorted by groomsmen. My impish five-year-old nephew, Stephen, was the pageboy. Jim and I defied tradition and walked down the aisle together: I didn't want one man handing me over to another like a piece of property.

My father welcomed everyone. "The introduction to the wedding service begins, 'We are gathered together,' but on this occasion there are many people who are not gathered with us. There's Joy's Uncle Chris in New Zealand. There are other members of your family, Jim, that would love to be here. And there are many friends from all over the world who would be here if they possibly could. One of them is a friend of Jim's, a priest from the Philippines. Karl writes this, 'On October 25 at 1:00 p.m., or its equivalent time on this side of the globe, I will light a candle in the chapel up in the mountains and say a prayer for Joy and Jim, and perhaps even sing a song of praise that will echo across the mountain range....' "

Greeting our friends after the wedding ceremony.

My father lit a candle. "In a few moments of silence, let us imagine his voice across the mountains and join in spirit with those who can't be here today."

A short time later as we stood at the side of the church, signing the registers, I noticed tears in my mother's eyes and a big smile on her face. I followed her gaze and saw that my Uncle Chris, who was supposed to be in New Zealand, had slipped in the back of the church. What a wonderful surprise.

When the ceremony was over, we immediately cut the cake and opened the champagne for all who were there. Dawn and Lenny graciously signed autographs for the delighted children and teenagers and then posed for the press photographers who had tracked us down.

The Indian curry reception that followed delighted those who appreciate the delicious flavors of Indian cuisine found in abundance in London. One of Jim's groomsmen, Roy from California, was unfortunately quite unsure what to make of it. Roy is a man of great taste and style and had generously provided all four of the groomsmen with beautiful matching waistcoats. His disappointment over the food was compensated by the fact that he sat close to a friend of mine who fascinated him. A little while later, at the dance party, we noted that both of them had disappeared!

The colored lights were flashing in time to the music as my brother, Ray, and his son, Jacob, used their DJ expertise to warm up the crowd. They didn't need much encouragement. We had invited a great crowd to dance and party with us in the church hall, and it was a blast.

We had been a little worried about how Jim's parents would feel about the dancing part of the wedding. Jim and Phyllis Wallis had founded a congregation of the conservative evangelical church called Plymouth Brethren. That church is well known for its disapproval of certain things like dancing and drinking. They had mellowed over the years, but would this be a little too much for them to take?

We had set aside a quiet lounge for people who wanted to talk, expecting that Jim's parents would want to be in there. But no! They never moved from the dance hall, enjoying every minute. "Phyllis," commented Jim's dad, "they seem to know all the words to these songs!"

As Jim and I happily watched the scene, I noticed a friend of mine moving toward Jim's dad as she danced. She had drunk too much and was on a mission. She stood in front of Jim Senior's chair and grabbed his hand. "Come on, darlin," she called down to him, "come and have a dance with me." Without waiting for an answer, she pulled him onto the dance floor. She gyrated around

At my marriage to Jim on October 25, 1997, with Dawn French, in a wonderful big hat, and her husband, Lenny Henry.

him pulling him back and forth as Hot Chocolate sang "You Sexy Thing." We were open-mouthed. Jim's dad had a bemused smile on his face and he moved with her as best he could. Soon he began to enjoy himself, and Phyllis joined him on the dance floor.

Jim's brother, Bill, watching with delight, yelled, "Quick! Someone get a camera." It was a wonderful moment for Jim and his brother and sister to see their parents so happy and dancing.

When it was time for Jim and me to leave the party, all the guests made an enormous tunnel, as men on one side and women on the other joined hands over their heads. Music played and Jim and I passed through the tunnel hugging and kissing our friends. I was kissing them goodbye and the sorrow of that mingled strangely with my joy.

As we climbed into the car, my brother threw his golf clubs into the back, and I eyed Jim suspiciously. The driver had instructions to take us to a secret destination, a gift from my family. They had booked us into the glorious Selsdon Park Hotel, complete with golf course, for one night. As the car pulled away from the waving crowd, my brother-in-law John, who has spina bifida, held on to the tow bar and rode behind us in his wheelchair. Thanks to my brother, on the first day of our married life together, I accompanied my husband as he played eighteen holes of golf.

By the next day, we were honeymooning in Cyprus, lazing beside a hotel pool. We chuckled as we saw the Brits on either side of us reading about our wedding and looking at our picture with Dawn French and Lenny Henry in the *Daily Mail*. Little did they know that the people in the pictures were sitting beside them sunbathing.

In November, I moved to Washington and into the house where Jim lived, in the northwest quarter of the District. Because I was an ordained priest in the Church of England, which is in turn a part of the wider Anglican Communion, I was able to transfer to the Episcopal Church of the USA, known as ECUSA. Upon receiving a very positive reference from the bishop of Southwark, the bishop of Washington, D.C., happily granted me a license to work in his diocese.

The people of Grace Church in Georgetown had been hoping that I would return after my few months with them, and it was with a deep sense of gratitude that I began work as the associate rector at Grace Church. Not only was I grateful to have been given a job; I was grateful that I could continue to do overseas what I had felt called by God to do.

The year that followed brought so many changes in my life, I felt as though I was reinventing myself. At least I was still able to be a priest in the Anglican Church. In marrying Jim, I had not only found a partner with whom I was madly in love, but one through whom my horizons were broadened beyond imagining. Jim has a long history as a leading, prophetic voice for progressive Christians who are concerned that faith should find its fundamental expression in practice, that is, reflected in our communities and politics. The magazine that he runs is called *Sojourners,* and is one of the few Christian publications that aims to address issues having to do with faith, politics, and culture.

Many in America had been led to believe that the only political voice for Christians was the religious right: the Moral Majority, or the Christian Coalition. Jim represents an alternative Christian voice, one that says not all Bible-believing Christians believe the same things as these people. Both *Sojourners* magazine and Call to Renewal, an organization that unites churches in the fight to overcome poverty, are a light in the darkness of American religious and political injustice.

In Daytona Beach, Florida, there is a motel called El Caribe, which has become a special place for me. Jim has been there many times over the years, and now I have too. He took several weeks at a time to write books there in his days as a single man. In recent years, he also made the popular move of holding Call to Renewal annual board meetings there. Mary Ann Richardson, the owner of the El Caribe, is a wonderful friend to Jim, his work, and our family, and the place has become a bolt-hole for both our work and vacations.

It was January 1998, and Jim and I had been married for three months. We were at the El Caribe for a board meeting. When it was over, Jim and I took a long walk along the beautiful stretch of beach. You could see for miles, and we walked and walked. The waves crashed onto the sand, and the sandpipers dashed back and forth, frantically searching for food before the next wave reached their fast little feet. As the sun set, and the waves crashed onto the sand, our conversation turned to whether or not we wanted children — and if we did, then when?

We both agreed that we would love to be parents if it were possible. "If it's not possible for us to have kids, I'd be very sad," I said, "but we have each other and extremely interesting lives ahead. I already feel blessed beyond belief."

"If it is possible, the question is 'When?' " said Jim.

"You have to remember that we are pretty old to be having kids. It may not be easy," I mused.

"Oh, I don't think we'll have any trouble," laughed Jim. "We're both fit and virile!"

I wasn't so sure. I had heard so many heartbreaking stories of people who couldn't conceive a baby.

"I think we should just let it happen when it happens, rather than wait. It could take a long time, and we can enjoy working at it," I said.

"Well, maybe," Jim replied. "Let's agree that we're both ready to be parents and be less careful in the spring. Getting pregnant six months to a year after being married would be ideal." We had made a big decision, and we gave each other a hug. As it turned out, at the time we were having that conversation on the beach, I was already a few weeks pregnant!

For some time, we had been planning to spend the following academic year at Harvard University in Cambridge, Massachusetts, where Jim had been invited to teach. Jim would be a fellow at the Center for the Study of Values in Public Life, at the Divinity School. I was looking forward to living in the quaint and bustling university town.

I'd found a small apartment for us to rent on the campus of the Episcopal Divinity School, and we took a few bare essentials to make it feel like home. In addition, we had to make arrangements for our baby to be born in Boston. Jim was eager to get there as soon as possible. Our baby was due in September, and he had made a mental note of all the hospitals en route to Cambridge.

At eight months pregnant, the Washington heat and humidity were intense as we got ready for the big move to Harvard. We were towing a trailer behind our car for the ten-hour journey to Cambridge. I waddled around the house supervising the move, telling our friends what to load and what to leave. When the trailer was all packed and we were ready to go, we made one last visit to my gynecologist.

"Well?" Jim asked as I was examined. "Is she likely to give birth in the next twenty-four hours?" With all the assurances to the contrary that we needed, we climbed into the car for the long, uncomfortable journey north.

Our apartment in Cambridge wouldn't be available to us until the end of August, so for three weeks we were house sitters.

Some friends of a friend were away for the summer, and we were very grateful for a place to land and wait for our final move. Our temporary house was old and surrounded by trees, and felt very English to me.

One night we were lying in bed. At eight-and-a-half months pregnant, it had taken me a while to get comfortable with my huge bump. I was almost asleep when I was startled by a fluttering sound. I opened my eyes, wondering if I had imagined it. Suddenly, something swooped across the front of my face with a very light flutter. Frantically, I scanned the room and saw the black shape hanging on the curtain rail. It took off again and this time I was in no doubt: it was a bat. I sat bolt upright and screamed, "Jim, Jim, it's a bat, Jim, wake up!" The little feet inside my tummy began to kick.

Jim rolled over and said, "It's okay, honey, it was just a dream, go back to sleep."

"No, no, it's not a dream. There's a bat in here. Get it out! Get it out! I have to get out...." I was almost hysterical. I heaved myself out of bed and made a dash for the bathroom. I checked behind the shower curtain and then shut the door tight. Sitting on top of the toilet seat, I called out to Jim. "Jim, I'm really sorry, but I can't help with this. Bats scare me, and I'm not coming out of here until it's out of the house."

My brave husband turned on all the lights and found an old tennis racquet in a closet. He leaped around in his boxer shorts chasing the bat as it fluttered around the house. He didn't want to kill it and wasn't sure how to corner or handle a bat, so he called the local police and asked their advice. The police officer on the other end of the phone was very helpful. "If you corner a bat, it might try to attack, so the best thing to do is open the windows of a bedroom and try to get the bat in there. Close the door and it will eventually fly out of the window." It worked! Jim managed to get the bat into the room with an open window and, by morning, it was gone. Now that our son Luke is three, he loves to hear me tell the story of the bat that came into our bedroom when he was a baby inside mummy's tummy. Jim and I have to tell it over and over again. On one long car journey, Luke had us tell him about the bat more than thirty times!

Just before the end of August, we moved into our cozy apartment at the Episcopal Divinity School, and I felt good. Cambridge was a beautiful place to be. With all the trees and commons, bookshops and students, I was reminded of English university towns. What a lovely place to spend nine months with a new baby.

Jim was all set to begin his year as a research fellow at Harvard University. He had driven several dummy runs to the hospital and we had found a new doctor — all just in time. At 9:30 a.m. on Thursday, September 3, my waters broke in our little bathroom.

"Mum, it's ten days early but I'm in labor!" I clutched the phone with excitement. My mother was due to come and stay with us when Luke was born, but her ticket to fly was for the next week. She packed her bag and went with Dad to the airport. The airline took pity on the expectant grandma, and a few hours later she was on her way from London to Boston.

I was writing a monthly column for *Christianity* magazine in England, and my next article was due. Jim came to the rescue and wrote it for me. It summed up just how we felt.

"At 6:56 p.m., September 3, 1998, Luke Carroll Wallis came into the world. Seven pounds, seven ounces and twenty inches long were the vital statistics. More vital was a healthy baby who entered the world without distress in a good, natural labor, sporting lots of dark hair and big, blue eyes.

"Luke went straight to his mother's breast and to his happy parents' hearts. This first week of Luke's life has been full of pure delights. Helping him learn to feed, watching him sleep, giving him his first bath, getting to know every part of his little body, taking him out for his first walk and enjoying people's smiles and attention, wondering about his future, smiling at each other a lot. These have been the initial wonders for Joy and me. Our world is full of light at the moment. Having a baby is the most common thing in the world. Yet, each little part of welcoming this new life into your life seems so unique and special to the parents and family involved. That's common grace. It is, indeed, a gift from God, and nothing makes us more aware of how precious God's gifts are than a newborn baby. Life itself seems more precious to us right now than it ever has before; an almost universal experience for parents.

"Perhaps that's why, when we see little babies threatened by famine, war, or extreme poverty, our hearts go out. This is not supposed to be. Everything in you wants to protect and nurture that child. You didn't really know that, in addition to each other, you could love someone else so much, and so immediately. It's a powerful feeling as new parents, and one, we suspect, that God has a great deal to do with.

"We walked all around the beautiful campus of the Episcopal Divinity School yesterday, on a perfect fall day. All the new students were having their orientation, just as we were having ours as new parents. We wandered into the empty chapel, and I realized it was Luke's first time in church. When I saw the pulpit, I couldn't resist climbing up there with Luke nestling in the baby carrier against my chest. I guess I just wanted him to get used to being in a pulpit — you know, just in case. I thought he seemed remarkably comfortable. Joy noted that he was asleep, as people often are in church.

"Holding him in the delivery room, I did pray as many parents do that Luke would be everything that God desires of him and created him to be. Offering your child to God is a way of offering yourself to God again, and it felt that way to me. For the religious and not, there is a powerful spirituality in the birth of a child. Already, we're learning a little about the unconditional love of God for us through the way we feel about our own child. Through one of the most universal human experiences, parent after parent is taught the lessons of love and life. And all is grace."

I SPENT THE NEXT FEW WEEKS in a state of wonder at this little miracle. I cried at the drop of a hat, feeling overwhelmed by how much love I felt so immediately for our little boy. It was unconditional and sacrificial love; in becoming a mother, I began to understand a bit more of what God's love for us is like.

When Luke was two weeks old, we took him on his first outing. It was a beautiful autumn day in Cambridge. Mum, Jim, Luke, and I walked over to join twenty-five thousand others gathered in Harvard Yard to hear Nelson Mandela speak. Jim had been at Mandela's inauguration and had met him when he first came to America. He wanted his son to meet him too.

Mandela was receiving an honorary doctorate from the university. He was the third person in history to receive this award — the other two were George Washington and Winston Churchill. Two-week-old Luke slept in his stroller while the eighty-year-old president of South Africa spoke to the awestruck crowd. I noted not only the humble integrity of the man but also the contrast I saw when compared to the man who was then president of the United States. I was tired of hearing about Bill Clinton and his escapades. I was bored by the endless political analysis on the American TV screens. To be in the presence of a trusted, respected, and true moral political leader was refreshing.

The following Sunday, we went to church at the Harvard Memorial Chapel. In his sermon, the minister Peter, Gomes, said of Mandela, "This is a man who knows who he is. His ideals are intact. He doesn't live with the illusions of his demons. He does not stagger at the uneven motions of the world." One day, Jim and I will tell Luke about this great man, Mandela, and how they overlapped in history in Harvard Yard.

There was another person with whom Luke's life overlapped for eight brief months: his grandmother, Phyllis Wallis. Jim's mum had been dancing at our wedding. A month later, she discovered that she had cancer of the stomach lining.

Thus began for Phyllis a long battle. She fought the disease with a combination of conventional surgery, chemotherapy and alternative treatments of vitamins, serums, and an extremely healthy diet. At one point, she drank so much carrot juice that she actually turned orange. She was so strong and determined that she also survived a heart attack and heart surgery, twice. It was a great thrill and joy for her to get to know Luke, her thirteenth grandchild.

Soon Phyllis had another goal to live for. Jim's sister, Marcie, was pregnant. Phyllis was expecting grandchild number fourteen on the day before her seventy-fifth birthday in May. She battled on, looking more and more healthy after each setback.

Then suddenly, one weekend in April, Jim and I got a call from his brother in Detroit. Phyllis had collapsed in the bathroom with an infection in her bloodstream. I have since discovered that four out of five cancer patients die from something other than the cancer itself, because the body has been so weakened by treatment.

Two days later we were at her hospital bedside, doctors fearing she might not live through the night.

Meanwhile, Marcie had gone into the early stages of labor. Though she was at home and a two-hour drive away, she made a quick and brave decision to drive to the hospital where her mother lay fighting for her life. Marcie had her medical notes faxed to the hospital in Detroit and then, with her husband and three children in tow, drove to have her baby in the same hospital with her mum.

The next morning, on Phyllis's seventy-fifth birthday, Marcie went into serious labor. They were two women on a mission: Phyllis labored for her life with each breath; Marcie labored to bring forth new life. On the first floor of the hospital, Kaylee Ruth was born, while on the fifth floor her grandmother Phyllis Ruth lay dying.

As soon as possible, the hospital staff wheeled Marcie and the baby into Phyllis's room, where we were all so anxiously waiting. The jubilation was overwhelming. The whole hospital had been following the drama and willing these two special people to meet. As Phyllis held her granddaughter she smiled and then spoke her last words, "I'm very happy, I'm very, very happy."

Then she slipped into a coma. Both the doctor and nurse who helped Marcie deliver were in the room, in tears like the rest of us. The veteran obstetrician later remarked that he had never been involved in a birth story so extraordinary. Phyllis never came out of the coma and died a few days later.

We all witnessed the grace of God that week: the paschal mystery of life and death, literally side by side. The grieving of Phyllis Ruth's passing and the joy of Kaylee Ruth's birth filled our hearts with tears of sorrow and of joy. I have never experienced a more vivid illustration of death and resurrection bound together by the love of family and the love of God. This hope of life in the midst of death is what the Christian faith is all about.

Chapter Thirteen

Culture Shock

I poured a glass of lemonade and moved slowly up the stairs to the bedroom with Luke crawling in front of me. By the time we reached the door, we were soaked with sweat. I opened it and breathed a sigh of relief as the cool air hit us. I knew that the summer months would be hot and humid in Washington, but nothing had quite prepared me for this summer of record high temperatures not reached since 1919. I was at home with a small child in a house with only one air-conditioning unit, in our bedroom.

For weeks, the dangerously hot temperature had hovered around 105°F. It was so hot that sections of highways buckled and the air was unhealthy to breathe. The city opened five "cooling stations" for people too exposed to the heat, and there were extreme weather warnings issued regularly on radio and TV, urging people to drink lots of water, to check on the elderly, and not to leave children or animals in closed cars while running errands. I was so thankful for our air-conditioned car and could hardly imagine surviving a summer driving around with a baby without the cool air. Jim and I reluctantly agreed

228

that the next year we would buy air conditioners for the whole house.

In 1914, Alexander Graham Bell asked, "If man has the intelligence to heat his house in the winter time, why does he not cool it in the summer?" Someone else said, "If they can cool dead dogs in Chicago, why not people in the New York Stock Exchange?" Air conditioning made sense, but at the same time I couldn't help but wonder whether technology's greatest comfort hadn't been a big contribution to a relentless, work-crazy, consumer society.

Before air conditioning existed, people must have lived and worked at a slower pace and, yes, achieved less. Before air conditioning, the Washington politicians left town from mid-June to September. Now they stay around with no break in their mischief making.

On days when we simply had to escape the heat of the house and the confines of the bedroom, where did we, and millions of other Americans spend the day? Not at the beach or in the park, nor at the pool or in the yard — all were too hot. We went to the comfort of a big, air-conditioned shopping center, complete with movie theaters and food courts to spend more money and buy more things!

The heat wasn't the only thing that turned out to be a challenge for me. It's true that the British and Americans speak the same language, but for this English newcomer to the "land of the free," there were a number of culture shocks in store. In the beginning, it was the little things that were the greatest challenge. Driving on the right-hand side of the road was relatively easy, but parking on the street outside our house was a complex affair. Until I got used to the signs telling me which hours of which days I was allowed to park, I must have paid several hundred dollars in parking tickets. Securing an American driver's license and the registration documents needed for the car required very little proof of driving ability but an enormous amount of skill and patience in navigating the red tape of the District's Department of Motor Vehicles.

I slowly figured out how to live in Washington. As I learned more about the place in which I was living, the deeper cultural differences between our two countries became more apparent. A country's culture strongly affects the way its people think, the way they believe, and the way they do politics.

There were basically three things that made my blood boil about America, and they are still the three things that would drive me home to England in an instant if Jim's work and calling didn't keep us here. Let me stand on my soapbox for a while and pontificate.

It was a cold winter night's and Luke snuggled beside me with his blanket as I read him bedtime stories. "Want Daddy ... " he murmured as I began the second story.

"Daddy's on a trip," I replied. "We'll call him in a few minutes and you can say goodnight to him, Okay?"

"Okay," he smiled settling back down. He was getting used to Daddy being on trips, and he knew he always came home after a day or two bearing gifts.

Suddenly, gunshots rang out on the street outside. This was the second time I had heard them in recent months, but never so close. I heard yelling and dashed to the window. Outside I could see teenagers running around the corner; one holding a gun.

Grabbing the phone, I dialed 911, the emergency services. No one answered. On my mobile phone, I called Jim. "There's shooting going on outside. What shall I do?" I asked quickly when he answered the phone. "Get

Luke and move away from the window," he said calmly. By this time the place was swarming with police. Helicopters with searchlights hovered overhead and officers crawled through our front and back yards. Someone had been killed. It wasn't the first time I had experienced this, and it wasn't to be the last.

In the days following the shootings, I worried a lot about bringing Luke up in a neighborhood like ours in Washington. But I soon came to realize that, no matter where children live and go to school in the United States, they risk being shot. I was staggered by the availability and accessibility of guns to children.

We had a student working as an intern for Jim in the summer. She was from Mississippi and lived in our basement apartment. Through talking to her I began to get a picture of American gun culture. "Joy, where I come from, most kids get their first guns at around seven years old" — for hunting, she assured me.

I began to realize that, in America, it would be impossible to ban guns in people's homes, as is the case in Britain. My friend from Mississippi explained: "The right to bear arms is a deeply rooted part of American culture. It has to do with a sense of personal freedom and civil liberty. Many see it as a necessary protection, either from criminals or totalitarian government."

Then, with horrifying regularity, I began to hear the news that children were on the rampage killing each other — and other people — in middle-class, suburban schools. Places like Littleton, Colorado, Jonesboro, Arkansas, and Comer, Georgia. People argued about who or what was to blame. Was it the fault of the media, the parents, or the guns? It seemed obvious to me that all three should be held accountable to some degree.

Violent TV shows and video and computer games are
big time in America. The parents who allow their kids
unlimited and uncontrolled access to them are equally responsible. I heard a minister who conducted one of the
memorial services for a slain youth say, "Lack of disci-
pline is a form of child abuse." I agreed. "But," I said to
many friends in the United States, "we have violent American movies in England. Our kids also have too much
exposure to violent TV and games and, of course, we also
have parents who allow their kids too much access to it
all, but they don't shoot each other, because they don't
have guns! Who can deny that if the guns weren't readily
available, the kids would not be dying." Charlton Hes-
ton, the actor whom we ironically remember as Moses in
The Ten Commandments, chairs the gun lobby. I got very
angry at their slogan, "Guns don't kill, people do."

After the shooting in Dunblane, Scotland, tough new
gun laws were established in Britain, and hunters had
to lock up their rifles in gun clubs when they were not
hunting. Recently, in America, Bill Clinton suggested new
gun laws that would restrict people to buying only one
handgun per month!

Before the Littleton killings, Colorado was on the verge
of lifting restrictions on carrying concealed weapons,
which would have allowed Denver Broncos football fans
to bring their guns along with them to the game. Imagine
guns at a Liverpool v. Millwall football match.

Luke was just one year old when he went with his
mum to his first anti-gun rally. It was "The Million Mom
March" in Washington, where a million mums gathered
to speak out against the weapons of violence that kill their
children in so many ways.

ANOTHER NEW EXPERIENCE in America was the healthcare system. Each month we, like many other Americans, paid a sum of money to a healthcare provider to insure a fairly comprehensive level of care, but there were exceptions. Fortunately, my condition was not serious or life threatening. Washington is sometimes referred to as the allergy capital of the world and, indeed, hay fever hit me with a vengeance. When my doctor prescribed the drug that would be most effective, I was dismayed to discover that I would have to pay more than $100 for it as opposed to the usual $5 charge because our health providers would pay only for drugs they chose. I went with the cheaper option and simply suffered a little more with a less effective medication that my insurance deemed to cover. Unless patients could pay extra-high prices, not all treatment was available to them; and worse, insurance companies decided what was appropriate treatment rather than doctors.

What happens to people who can't afford the health insurance payments in the first place? The very poor, I was relieved to learn, are in fact provided for with a government insurance called Medicaid. But the dreadful truth is that there are 44 million people, often referred to as the "working poor," who are not poor enough to receive Medicaid, but not rich enough to afford health insurance. A frightening statistic is that more than ten million children have no health cover age in America. For the uninsured, the only healthcare available is in a hospital emergency room (what we call "casualty" in England). Even then, it has been known for uninsured people to be turned away and sent to other hospitals, dying on the way. The film *John Q*, starring Denzel Washington, attempts to address this issue.

After my allergy came my teeth. I have always needed a lot of work done on them and, throughout my life, have spent more time visiting the dentist than the doctor. When I was a seminary student in Durham, I had my wisdom teeth removed under sedation at Sunderland General Hospital. As I waited for the surgery, the dental surgeon came and sat beside my bed. "Joy, as well as removing your impacted wisdom teeth, I will be removing an infected molar. I would like your permission to try an experiment. I want to put one of the good wisdom teeth that we take out into the hole left by the infected molar."

"You want to do a tooth transplant?" I was fascinated.

The dentist was honest, "It may last a month, it may last five years, I don't know, but I think it's worth trying."

"Okay," I said. "Let's give it a go."

I had wires in my mouth for a month and drank soup for weeks but, fourteen years later, it's still there. My other teeth haven't always been so well behaved, and I wasn't surprised when my dentist in Washington told me that I needed some crown work.

I patiently went through the same horrible experience that I have endured many times before, but the real pain came when the receptionist gave me the bill. I looked at the piece of paper and almost fainted. It was two thousand dollars. "But our health insurance covers 40 percent of dental work," I said hopefully. "The 40 percent has already been deducted," she smiled.

Since we were in the process of getting a mortgage to buy our house, I had no choice but to add two thousand dollars to the amount borrowed: my teeth are literally mortgaged! It suddenly became clear to me why so many of the poor people in my neighborhood have bad teeth and toothless grins.

THEN THERE ARE the differences in church. As a priest from the Church of England, licensed by the bishop in Washington, D.C., I am often asked by people on both sides of the Atlantic, "What differences do you see between the Church of England and the Episcopal Church in the USA?"

The Church of England is the established, state church. Every inch of the country is part of an Anglican parish, and everyone has a local church somewhere nearby, even if they don't attend it. Many people who hardly ever go to church would still see the Church of England as their church, simply because they are English.

The community expects the local parish church to "hatch, match, and dispatch," or "baptize, marry, and bury." In the course of a year as a local priest in England, I would conduct over a hundred funerals, several weddings, and a large number of baptisms. We belonged to, and were there to serve, the whole parish community. There are other denominations, of course, but they are in the minority and are sometimes referred to as the "nonconformists."

It shouldn't have surprised me that the Episcopal Church in America was very different in that respect. The pioneers had come to America to escape the Church of England and find religious freedom. They found it! There are thousands of Christian denominations in the United States, and more being created every day. The Episcopal Church is not the main denomination, but a smaller denomination among many. However, since the English colonists were Anglicans, the Episcopal Church remains disproportionately influential in the areas of the original colonies such as Virginia and Massachusetts.

When it comes to choosing a church, people want to
see the menu on offer. The idea of prioritizing attendance
at a local church is quite foreign. Most people in America
commute to church. They choose a church for the youth
program, the preacher, the choir, the organ, the liturgy,
or the kind of people who go there. Many denomina-
tional churches, including the Episcopal Church, have the
characteristics of a small club.

In the Episcopal Church, many like to think that it represents the historic Anglican tradition both in its music
and style. Some Anglophiles want it to be just like they
imagine the Church of England to be. Unfortunately, the
Church of England that most of them imagine is about
fifty years out of date. In the Church of England, I found
variety, flexibility, experimentation, and breadth of expression. On the East Coast of America, the hallmarks of
the Episcopal Church are excellence in traditional church
music, liturgy, and form. If anyone wants something more
up-to-date or different, they may be politely told to see
one of the many other churches on offer.

One Sunday, when covering for a rector who was away,
I played a track from a CD while people were receiving
communion. The words were particularly relevant to the
theme of the day, and the music was meditative. When
the rector returned he said, "Joy, I think people really enjoyed having you here last week. I've had several positive
comments on your sermon, but some people did com-
plain about your using a CD during communion. They
couldn't understand why you needed to do that when we
have such a fine organ. So perhaps you should avoid that
in the future."

In the past, the Episcopal Church was known as the denomination for the elite. While it is working to be rid of

this image, its members are still mainly white and upper-middle-class. One of the things I most enjoyed about the Church of England was that, where a neighborhood was mixed economically and racially, the membership of the church in that neighborhood often reflected that same diversity. It is rare in America to find a stable racially and economically diverse neighborhood, let alone a church like that in the middle of it.

Another disappointing difference between the Church of England and the Episcopal Church is that the Episcopal Church is firmly rooted in the economic culture of the United States. In the Church of England, all churches pay their quota to their respective diocese each year. The amount they pay depends on the location of the church, the size, and the combined average income of the congregation. Small, inner-city congregations pay a smaller amount than large suburban ones. In accord with a policy called "Fairer Shares," the diocese then provides all the churches of the diocese, whatever their size, with a clergy person and their housing. Inevitably — and I think fairly — the smaller, poorer churches receive much more than they give to the diocese, and the more wealthy parishes pay out more in quota than they receive back from the diocese. It generally works very well. And all the clergy get paid the same amount, regardless of where they serve.

In the United States, each church holds its own budget and can pay over and above the recommended amount for their clergy. This has several unhappy consequences. The wealthiest congregations can secure the best clergy, while churches that might be full of low-income people cannot afford to exist at all. Church growth in the Episcopal Church is therefore concentrated in comfortable, mainly white, middle-class neighborhoods.

Each church depends on the financial pledges of its members to run its programs and pay the clergy. This often results in power struggles where the wealthiest members or donors see the church as their property. Threats to withdraw pledges if the minister does something they don't like are not uncommon. Therefore, the priest's ability to lead or influence change can be unduly countermanded by the wealthy.

There are, however, several "downtown" churches, with significant outreach ministries to the poor and homeless, that have attracted me. One of the most impressive programs that I saw in action was that of the DC Central Kitchen. Not only did it provide food for the homeless community in the city, it enabled men and women climbing out of their desperate situations to contribute constructively to help themselves and others.

When my friend Carol Feneley, a founder of the program, showed me around DC Central Kitchen, I saw previously homeless men and women being trained and training others in the catering business. Beautiful platters of intricately cut vegetables and delicious meals had been prepared to the highest standards. As they worked with pride, I could see that the whole project gave meaning and incentive to the lives of the participants. They were not only being helped out of a mess, but also being trained and equipped to move on and make a valuable contribution to society. On occasions when Jim's office at *Sojourners* magazine has need for catering, a board lunch, or a special party, they always call the kitchen to do the catering. It is good value and provides delicious and well-prepared food.

The director of DC Central Kitchen was a member of Grace Church, where I was the associate rector, and the church was one of many that offered volunteer help and support. One of the things that I most appreciated about the outreach ministry of Grace Church was that some members were prepared to offer practical help as they joined with the Salvation Army on its soup runs to the cold and hungry on the streets. Once a month, I joined volunteers on the van that went out every night in the winter months. Wrapped up warmly, we drove around the nation's capital city and stopped at the places where the homeless slept. They were usually huddled around the large grates that emitted steam from the enormous heating systems of the city. The grates provided temporary warmth but soon made blankets damp and unhealthy.

Many have recognized that there is a need to go beyond the soup-run kind of outreach. The matters that cause the problems in the first place need to be addressed, whether it is bad government policy or bad patterns of behavior. Jim has launched an organization called Call to Renewal. Its aim is to unite all kinds of churches to overcome poverty. When speaking, he often says, "We are busy pulling drowning people out of the river, but what we need to do is go upstream and find out who is pushing them in." More and more partnerships are emerging between those who make policy and those who work on the ground, and the hope is that, one day, the incredible gap between the rich and the poor in America will be closed.

THE FACT THAT I AM ABLE to visit my friends and family twice a year has helped me deal with the culture shock of moving to America and so many life changes. In 1999, I was especially looking forward to going home for a reunion of friends who hadn't been all together for many years. Back in the early 1980s, when we were hanging out together at St. Luke's Church and drinking in the Hornes Tavern, someone had said, "Why don't we promise each other that, on the ninth day of the ninth month in 1999, we'll meet up? Wherever we are in the world, we'll meet at 9:00 a.m. in Trafalgar Square." It seemed such a long time away, and a cool idea. Two Christmases before the agreed date, my brother put notes in his Christmas cards, "Don't forget 9/9/99. See you there!"

I flew to England with Luke and could hardly wait. On September 9, I took the train into town and discovered how difficult it is to travel on the train and subway with a stroller and baby when you are on your own. It was a gloriously sunny autumn day and I felt a wave of sheer joy wash over me as I walked with Luke past St. Martin in the Fields Church and crossed the road into Trafalgar Square. Luke had just turned one and was delighted by the sights, the sounds, and the masses of pigeons. Nelson on his column looked down and the enormous stone lions looked on as another day in their long history began. I glanced at my watch and my heart skipped a beat as Big Ben chimed nine times.

I was the first to arrive and was approached by someone from another group who had had the same plan: "Are you waiting for the medical division of the Army in Germany reunion?"

"No," I smiled and walked around to the other side of the square.

Suddenly I saw them. The group included my old housemate, Nicky, with her husband and new baby, five old members of the group "One Way" that I sang with, some youth club friends, and my brother. Even Steve Nunney, my old flame who had been stabbed in the heart, had made it from the north of England.

We had a fabulous day. We took a boat ride down the River Thames and had a picnic in Greenwich Park. It wasn't long before we were laughing at old memories and marveling at how much we had and hadn't changed.

In the evening we met again, at 9:00 p.m. at the same place, and a few more were added to our number. With the kids that we had between us safe in the care of my parents, we enjoyed the great atmosphere of a lively Tex-Mex restaurant perfectly situated a short stroll from Trafalgar Square. The management knew why we were there and at the end of our meal presented us with delicious brownies that were specially decorated with sparklers, with "9/9/99" written on the top in chocolate.

After two years of living in America, England still felt like home and the place of my roots. But a whole new experience of the world was opening up before, me and having had such a happy time remembering my past, I went back to America to embrace again my new home and wonderful family.

Chapter Fourteen

September 11

Luke was three years old on September 3, 2001. We had just returned from Florida, where he had spent several weeks splashing around in the ocean and digging in the sand. The vacation was the kind that happy childhood memories are made of. Luke rode go-karts and beach motorbikes with his dad. With his cousins, he sped down water chutes and rode the lazy river rides until they closed the water park for the night. We walked on the beach with a flashlight at night and built great big sandcastles for smashing down during the day. Luke's favorite place was the pool where he swam like a fish. "Watch me!" was his constant cry as he showed anyone who was willing to watch how well he could swim under the water. On the long drive home, Jim and I talked a lot about the sense of calling I have had for a while, to plant a new church in our inner-city neighborhood of Washington.

Back home, Luke's birthday party was the highlight of his week. His friends from preschool joined him at a local park for a picnic, carousel rides, and a puppet show. As the children devoured the dinosaur cake that his god-mother had made, Jim and I looked on contentedly. We were very happy with, and proud of, our growing boy.

In the week that followed, we returned to work. Luke went back to school, where he was now in the "bumble-bee class" for three days a week. Jim went back to the *Sojourners* magazine office and his work with Call to Renewal. I returned to managing our home, entertaining guests, and writing my book, as well as doing preparation work for the new church that we were planning.

On Tuesday, September 11, I woke up to the sound of little footsteps pattering down the hallway. Our bedroom door burst open and Luke climbed into bed with us for a cuddle. "What shall we do today, Luke?" I asked. Usually I took him to the park to play, but only after we had run our errands for the day. I was a member of a wholesale cash and carry warehouse and needed to fill up the freezer with meat and buy toilet paper.

"I want to watch *Mary Poppins!*" he cried enthusiastically. "Well, how about we do that later, after we've done the shopping?" The store was at a shopping center called Pentagon City, right next door to the Pentagon, the U.S. government's military headquarters. Luke liked to drive over the 14th Street Bridge and wave to Mr. Jefferson inside his monument on the way to the store. Luke reluctantly agreed to postpone *Mary Poppins,* and we went downstairs to breakfast.

Jim was in the bathroom with the volume on the radio turned up loud, so that he could hear the news while he took a shower. I put the kettle on for my cup of tea and poured a glass of grapefruit juice. I popped bread into the toaster and filled Luke's tippy cup with milk.

"Mum! I want to watch *Dragon Tales,*" called Luke from the living room. I turned on the TV. A news channel was reporting that a plane had crashed into one of the twin towers of the World Trade Center in New York. "Oh, no!"

I gasped. "What, Mummy?" asked Luke. "A plane has just crashed into that building." Luke thought that was quite exciting and began to fly his toy plane into Lego towers.

I called up to Jim in the bathroom: "Turn your study TV on, it's terrible." He had already heard the news. We assumed it was a small aircraft that had somehow accidentally crashed into the World Trade Center. "Maybe the pilot had a heart attack," I wondered aloud. I changed the channel for Luke to watch his program and went upstairs to watch the news coverage with Jim in his study.

A gaping hole had appeared in Tower Number One, and smoke was spreading across the Manhattan skyline. Suddenly, we saw another plane crash into the second tower. It was a passenger plane. I looked at Jim in horror. His first words were "This is bad. This is really bad." It was immediately apparent that this was a terrorist attack and that the two planes had been hijacked on a suicide mission. Shortly after that, another plane crashed into the side of the Pentagon, and it felt like all hell was being let loose. A surge of panic came up through my stomach and stayed in my throat for days. Then we heard that another plane had crashed in the countryside in Pennsylvania.

Jim and I hovered around the TV, watching and waiting for what would come next. Jim was already late for work and, for a while, wasn't sure whether to stay with us or go to the office. Would we be safe? Should Luke and I go to the office too? We finally decided to stay at home while Jim went to the office. He needed to be there with his colleagues, reacting to this shocking news, and it seemed we were safe at home. We promised to talk every hour.

Our row house has a porch and a small front yard. Throughout the summer months we would sit and chat with our neighbors on both sides. Larry and Fran, an

African American couple with teenage kids, live on our right. On the left, Dave and Ashley, a young white couple, just moved in a year ago. Luke loves to sit on the stoop and call "Hi!" to passersby, often soaking everyone as he helps Ashley water her plants. On the morning of September 11, we all quickly gathered on our front porches: it was a ready-made support group. Dave had been evacuated from the city and cycled home. Larry had just taken his kids to school and came up the steps. "Everyone's going crazy out there," he said. "At the gas station on the corner, people are fighting to fill up their gas tanks to flee the city, shouting, 'We're being bombed!'"

We watched the traffic inch its way north out of the city. Public transport had been closed down, and some vehicles were packed with eight or more people. Others had just set off on foot and were walking hurriedly away from downtown. We had never seen anything like it. Some people at *Sojourners* set up tables to offer a cup of water to those walking home on that warm day.

I felt as though I was in the middle of a movie. I couldn't quite believe what had just happened. The shocking reality began to dawn on me as I listened to the reports of the attacks. Passengers on the hijacked planes had made calls to their loved ones on their cell phones and, as the world listened to their radios and watched their TVs, we began to get a terrifyingly clear picture of the events that had just transpired. Fear crept into my bones. For a while, no one could be sure that there weren't any more hijacked planes out there. It occurred to me almost immediately that if people were willing to die on these missions, then we must surely be vulnerable to chemical or germ warfare. The thought of being unable to protect Luke from that kind of harm added to the panic in my stomach.

I wanted to talk to my mum and dad but it was impossible to call almost anywhere, let alone out of the country. I knew they would be worrying, so I sent them an e-mail. It was only a few hours since the attack but, when I signed on, I had a whole bunch of e-mails from friends and family around the world with the simple message: "Are you all right?" The relief for them of hearing a "Yes, we're fine," was followed by an outpouring of anger, confusion, and compassion. My most primal instinct was to hold Luke close and keep him safe.

At the *Sojourners* office, Jim was working on a statement, just hours after the attack. He has an amazing ability to articulate what needs to be said in complex situations, and people around the world trust his good judgment and resonate with his words. This was a statement that thousands of religious leaders, from America's largest religious communities — Christian, Jewish, Muslim, and Buddhists — were to sign in the days ahead and was a valuable resource for clergy all over the world as they ministered to their concerned congregations. This is what it said:

Deny Them Their Victory:
A Religious Response to Terrorism

We, American religious leaders, share the broken hearts of our fellow citizens. The worst terrorist attack in history that assaulted New York City, Washington, D.C., and Pennsylvania, has been felt in every American community. Each life lost was of unique and sacred value in the eyes of God, and the connections Americans feel to those lives run very deep. In the face of such a cruel catastrophe, it is a time to look to God and to each other for the strength we need and the response we will make. We must dig deep to the roots of our faith for sustenance, solace, and wisdom.

First, we must find a word of consolation for the untold pain and suffering of our people. Our congregations will offer their practical and pastoral resources to bind up the wounds of the nation. We can become safe places to weep and secure places to begin rebuilding our shattered lives and communities. Our houses of worship should become public arenas for common prayer, community discussion, eventual healing, and forgiveness.

Second, we offer a word of sober restraint as our nation discerns what its response will be. We share the deep anger toward those who so callously and massively destroy innocent lives, no matter what the grievances or injustices invoked. In the name of God, we too demand that those responsible for these utterly evil acts be found and brought to justice. Those culpable must not escape accountability. But we must not, out of anger and vengeance, indiscriminately retaliate in ways that bring on even more loss of innocent life.

We pray that President Bush and members of Congress will seek the wisdom of God as they decide upon the appropriate response.

Third, we face deep and profound questions of what this attack on America will do to us as a nation. The terrorists have offered us a stark view of the world they would create, where the remedy to every human grievance and injustice is a resort to the random and cowardly violence of revenge — even against the most innocent. Having taken thousands of our lives, attacked our national symbols, forced our political leaders to flee their chambers of governance, disrupted our work and families, and struck fear into the hearts of our children, the terrorists must feel victorious.

But we can deny them their victory by refusing to submit to a world created in their image. Terrorism inflicts not only death and destruction but also emotional oppression to further its aims. We must not allow this terror to drive us away from being the people God has called us to be. We assert the vision of community, tolerance, compassion, justice, and the sacredness of human life, which lies at the heart of all our religious traditions. America must be a safe place for all our citizens in all their diversity. It is especially important that our citizens who share national origins, ethnicity, or religion with whoever attacked us are, themselves, protected among us.

Our American illusion of invulnerability has been shattered. From now on, we will look at the world in a different way, and this attack on our life as a nation will become a test of our national character. Let us make the right choices in this crisis — to pray, act, and unite against the bitter fruits of division, hatred, and violence. Let us rededicate ourselves to global peace, human dignity, and the eradication of injustice that breeds rage and vengeance.

As we gather in our houses of worship, let us begin a process of seeking the healing and grace of God.

In the following days, I only watched the news when Luke was at school or in bed. As I listened to the endless stories of people who had lost loved ones or died rescuing others,

I cried and cried. People all over the world are now familiar with the dreadful scenes and the thousands of moving
stories of loss and heroism.

One man interviewed had lost hundreds of his employees who worked at the World Trade Center on the 102nd
floor. He was late to work that morning because he had
taken his five-year-old daughter to her first day at school.
He described how he stood on the street watching in horror as the building burned and people ran out. "What
floor were you on?" he yelled to people as they passed
him. "The 58th," they replied. Then people came from the
60th. As they kept coming, he kept yelling "What floor
were you on?" Just as someone replied: "The 98th," the
whole tower collapsed. People fled to escape the cloud of
dust and rubble that rolled down the streets chasing them.
The tears rolled down his face and his voice broke as he
described what wonderful people these were. "I had seven
hundred employees. Now I have seven hundred bereaved
families."

Later, as I told Jim about these stories, I couldn't
help crying myself. Luke saw that I was upset and said,
"Mummy, are you sad because the plane crashed into the
building?" Then he hugged me. I hoped that he would not
be affected by all this and was especially careful to make
sure that he felt loved and secure. Whenever he did see
scenes of the rubble and destruction, I said, "Hey, Luke,
let's look for the helpers." He loves fire trucks and firefighters. It was a positive aspect of the whole nightmare
that he could focus on.

A few days later, as we were driving home from school,
the firefighters from Washington were on the streets col-
lecting money in their big boots for the families of those
firefighters who were killed. Luke was very excited about

putting his money into the boot and said to the firefighter, "Thank you for being a helper."

It was hard to let Jim go on his next trip, especially with the FBI issuing warnings from time to time for the public to be especially alert. They expected another attack of some kind. Airline crews were bravely going back to work and commanded a new respect from their passengers. Along with the police and emergency services, airline staff were elevated to a place of deep respect, admiration, and gratitude for the work they do.

On Saturday, September 15, on United Airlines Flight 564 out of Denver, a pilot gave a message to his passengers that was reported in the news:

> Sometimes a potential hijacker will announce that he has a bomb. There are no bombs on this aircraft and if someone were to get up and make that claim, don't believe him. If someone were to stand up, brandish something such as a plastic knife, and say, "This is a hijacking" or words to that effect, here is what you should do: Every one of you should stand up and immediately throw pillows, books, magazines, eyeglasses, shoes — anything that will throw him off balance and distract his attention. If he has a confederate or two, do the same thing with them. Most important: Get a blanket over him, then wrestle him to the floor and keep him there. We'll land the plane at the nearest airport and the authorities will take it from there. Remember, there will be one of him and maybe a few confederates, but there are two hundred of you. Now, since we're a family for the next few hours, I'll ask you to turn to the person next to you, introduce yourself, and ask them to do the same.

At the end of his address, Flight 564's passengers gave their pilot a round of applause.

In many ways, this unthinkable act of terrorism has brought out the best in many people, but not in all. Many innocent Americans, whose ethnic origins are from the Middle East, have been the victims of hate crimes. Muslims and mosques have been attacked; Muslim women have been afraid to leave their homes for fear of retribution; and many Arabic students in American universities have felt compelled to leave their courses and the country.

Racism is another form of attack on innocent people with dark skin. A friend of ours flew into the United States a week after the attack. She told us that all people of color in the immigration hall were shepherded to a separate line. Not one person complained about the racial profiling. There were, however, also encouraging acts of support for Muslim brothers and sisters. One Friday around noon, a worried American Muslim walked to his mosque for the weekly service. None of the Islamic females in the community had been able to attend out of fear. When he arrived, he was completely touched by what he found there. The mosque was surrounded by members of the wider community forming a human shield with white carnations in their hands. He said, "Tears came to my eyes, and I saw beautiful light shining through the darkness that has covered us this week. As we went in to worship, I said extra prayers that we were so lucky to be living with this kind of people. I have never felt as proud as an American Muslim as I did today. As goodness is not a monopoly for any one race or religion, neither is darkness."

Jim and I lit candles and said prayers. He preached sermons at many interfaith gatherings and prayer vigils in the next few weeks and spoke wise and prophetic words.

I myself went on a journey trying to figure out what I believed, thought, and felt about the events.

On several occasions, President George Bush made statements that indicated he had no idea why America was a target for the terrorists. At a press conference a month after the initial attack, he said he was amazed why anyone could be against what America stood for. Many people, to both the left and the right of the political and religious spectrum, were ready to come up with explanations. They blamed the attacks on the "sins of the nation" — each citing different sins, of course.

Two right-wing Christian fundamentalists made an astounding assertion. Speaking on Reverend Pat Robertson's TV show, *The 700 Club,* just two days after the attacks, the Reverend Jerry Falwell said that the United States got "probably what we deserved." "Jerry, that's my feeling," the Reverend Robertson replied.

Falwell continued, "I really believe that the pagans and the abortionists and the feminists and the gays and lesbians who are actively trying to make that an alternative lifestyle, the ACLU, People for the American Way — all of them who have tried to secularize America — I point the finger in their face and say, 'You helped this happen.'"

"I totally concur," said Robertson. How un-Christian, I thought, while one newspaper review noted that they sounded like the American Taliban.

Some left-wing commentators explained how America's foreign policies had made it the enemy of the Islamic world. For years, they said, when it suited its purposes the United States allied itself with terrorists such as Saddam Hussein, when Iran was the enemy, or even Bin Laden, when the Soviets were the enemy. America's backing of corrupt Gulf State regimes and its staunch support for

Israel, despite its brutal policies toward the Palestinian people, gave more cause to Middle Eastern hatred.

There is indeed a long litany of grievances against America that many people around the world understand. Yet nothing justifies terrorism, whether it is Israeli to Palestinian, Palestinian to Israeli, or terrorist to American. I believe it is simply wrong for anyone, politically left or right, to even imply that America deserved what it got; there was nothing "understandable" about the attacks on September 11.

As I GET USED TO LIVING in a country at war with terrorism, I am becoming accustomed to living on the edge of fear. Americans, and those of us who live here, are experiencing for the first time how it feels to be vulnerable and afraid. I hope it helps us to be more empathetic and compassionate toward other victims of violence all around the world.

Gandhi said that the best response to evil is a nonviolent one, but if that is not possible, the next best response would be violent resistance. The least appropriate response is to be passive in the face of evil. Some may say that this is a slippery slope and is the argument for those who support war. But life is full of slippery slopes. We need the gift of discernment and must take care not to fall, especially in times like this. I would like to see a genuine international response, where terrorists charged with crimes could be brought before an international tribunal. Such an international response might have more chance of success, and seem less arrogant.

In the sad and somber wake of September 11, the late-night American TV comedians were very careful and sensitive about the way they used humor. In the midst of all this caution, however, there was one suggestion that Bin Laden be covertly captured by the Special Forces and flown to an undisclosed hospital, where surgeons would quickly perform a complete sex-change operation on him. After that, she could be returned Afghanistan, to live as a woman under the Taliban....

I OFTEN ANNOY my American family and friends by being so pro-British and anti-American when it comes to the news. So, in some ways, my final reflection surprises even me. I have more affection for America now than I did before September 11. It is true that I am more nervous about living here, but I have been part of this nation coming together. It is impossible to remain untouched by the patriotic spirit of unity, rooted in grief and anger. People in this very individualistic country are learning what it means to be connected to and concerned for others. A unity is forming that reaches across the boundaries of class, race, and gender.

Needless to say, I have never felt patriotic toward America, but now I find myself stirred by emotion in the wake of the attacks. I am proud of the people who struggled to save others, who fought with hijackers on a plane, who sacrificed themselves for strangers, demonstrating the best of humanity. I have shed countless tears over the many stories of death and loss, over the children who lost their parents, over parents who lost their children. I have grieved with a nation. Just as you bond when you grieve with a friend, I have bonded a little more with the people of America.

Epilogue

"Please, God, send us a baby. Amen," This was Luke's most frequent prayer at night, at the dinner table, in the car, at church, and it echoed the desire of our hearts too. In fact, we had been doing our part for a couple of years. We'd had two miscarriages and were beginning to wonder if another child was meant to be for us. My book was written, Luke was about to start school full time and I began to ask God and myself what I should be doing next.

God may have been giving me a clue as my friends and neighbors began to say things like,

"Since 9/11, I'm not hearing the prophetic word of God being preached from the pulpit in my church."

"I go to a great alternative church that focuses on social justice, but there really isn't a place for my kids."

"The music in my church is so traditional; there's no room for a variety of styles."

"I'm a spiritual person but I'm not so sure about church...."

"I don't care about the denomination, I just want an integrated, authentic worship experience."

I too was feeling frustrated, mostly with the traditional prayer book liturgy of the Episcopal churches in Washington, D.C. And so a group of us got together and began to explore what it might look like if we created a worship experience that tried to meet some of those expressed needs.

What we ended up with was an ecumenical congregation committed to social justice through biblical prophetic preaching, creative liturgy, uplifting music, and kids. It attracted quite a diverse crowd, ranging from those who were on their way out of the church in despair to those who were seeking a way in.

This experiment of ours was an exciting one, and we wondered if it would be possible to become a mission church of the Episcopal Diocese of Washington, D.C. After much conversation, prayer, and searching for the way ahead, two things happened to give us the clarity we needed. First, I got pregnant! And, second, we could not overcome the fact that the canon laws of the Episcopal Church would not allow for a congregation, in which a non-Episcopal minister might at times celebrate the Eucharist. As a deeply committed Anglican, I understood the difficulty but felt disappointed. For the first time in my life, I was about to step back and let go for a while of my official engagement with the Anglican Church.

OPPORTUNITIES FOR MINISTRY, however, were abundant, with invitations to speak at a number of events, including some in England. I was in fact just a few weeks pregnant with my second son, Jack, when I danced with Rowan Williams, the man who was about to become the next archbishop of Canterbury. We were an elevated part of a crowd of thousands at the Greenbelt Christian arts festival in England. We had just concelebrated at the outdoor Eucharist as the August bank holiday weekend came to an end and the Celtic band began to play. Everyone it seemed rose to their feet to jig and dance, while Archbishop Rowan and I stood on a central podium trying to look dignified in our liturgical robes. All of a sudden a woman jumped up and grabbed our hands, "Come on and dance," she cried, and so we did. The next morning, the *Times* of London carried a photograph and wrote, "Dr. Williams took to the floor and danced a Scottish reel with the Rev. Joy Carroll, the woman priest who inspired the hit television series *The Vicar of Dibley.*"

I don't think there has been much dancing since then for the Archbishop of Canterbury, presiding over a communion that is in danger of schism. I wonder if it's like a parent trying to keep the family together when the siblings are fighting.

SIX MONTHS LATER, I still had a month to go before our baby was expected. Jim was out of town at a Call to Renewal Board meeting in Florida. Luke had a cough and was asleep in my bed. At 11:30 p.m. and quite unexpectedly, my water broke, Jack was on his way into the world and I was on my own with a sleeping four-year-old in the bed next to me. For half an hour I tried to get hold of Jim. He was speaking on his cell phone and his computer was plugged into the hotel phone jack. Finally, I had a hotel staffperson go knock on his door. "Your wife is on the phone and it's urgent..."

Jim soon mobilized our friends and began to make his way home as quickly as he could. He took a $150 taxi ride to Jacksonville airport, where he caught the earliest flight back to D.C. the next morning.

Within minutes other friends and neighbors were with me. One couple stayed the night with Luke, another friend drove me to the hospital, and another committed to stay with me until the baby was born. Fortunately my labor was slow and nothing much happened all night. Jim arrived at 8:00 a.m., and serious labor had not yet begun.

It was the eve of the war with Iraq, and Jim had been working very hard to try to stop it. Sojourners had just launched the 6-Point Plan, offered by U.S. church leaders as an alternative to war with Iraq, and in less than two weeks the plan had spread around the country and the world. Suddenly, right there in the labor and delivery room Jim's cell phone began to ring. On the other end were British cabinet ministers and members of Parliament who had seen the plan and were facing a Parliamentary debate the next morning. "Jim is this a good time to talk about the 6-Point Plan?" they asked. While the nurses looked horrified, I told Jim that he should take the calls and take his best shot at stopping the war. After all, what could he do? I wasn't pushing yet.

By the early afternoon Jackson was born. Just as we were taking him home from the hospital two days later, the war began. We were filled with a mixture of sadness that the war could not be stopped and sheer happiness over this new little life that had joined our family. What a poignant reminder of how precious life is at a time when so many were about to lose their lives amid the madness of war.

THE REALITY of having two children hit home when Jack was about six months old, and I realized that what I once heard network broadcaster Cokie Roberts say was true, "Women can have it all, but they can't have it all at once."

Today we gather once a month on a Sunday night for an ecumenical service of worship. "Sundays at Sojourners. Worshipping in the Spirit of Justice" is where I "keep my hand in" and find an outlet for my priestly vocation. But I have discovered that priesthood is unconfined. Whether or not the priest has a church, the vocation lives and finds expression. For me I have come to realize that the priestly part of my being goes with me into the playground after Luke's school day, it goes with me as I organize the five-year-olds' soccer team, it goes with me as we build a community of moms and dads who playfully call ourselves "the village" in our effort to raise our kids.

Those who are priests in secular employment have already discovered this, but I have been pleasantly surprised to find that I still exercise a priestly ministry outside the church, almost without intending to. I listen, I support, I encourage, I explain, I take initiatives, I am able to be there as a person, as a mom, as a Christian, and from time to time God uses all that.

When I was a parish priest, I remember the bishop explaining that we were paid a stipend as opposed to a salary. The stipend was a sum of money that enabled us not to work; it enabled us to be present to a community as a priest. This was quite liberating for me, that I was not being paid for my performance as a priest but was financially enabled by the diocese to "be" a priest in all its fullness.

THESE DAYS I feel thankful that I am able to "be" a "stay-at-home mom," and I wonder if anyone has ever been

Me with Jim and our son Luke, having dinner on vacation in San Francisco.

recognized as a "mommy priest" as opposed to a "worker priest."

Luke and I were watching *Harry Potter and the Philosopher's Stone* the other day. Near the end of the movie there is the big confrontation between Harry and Voldemort. Voldemort wants Harry to join his evil side and tries to tempt him with the promise that he will see his dead parents again. Voldemort says, "There is no good and evil, only power." Luke turned to me indignantly and said, "That's not true is it, Mum? Evil tells lies and good tells the truth." The complexities around all that can wait until he's older, but he's developing his value system, and I am glad to be able to help shape it. Parish priests have the "cure of souls" of those in their parish. I still have the "cure of souls," but it's more focused these days on the spiritual and social formation of our children.

Jim, Luke, Jack, and Joy at home during Christmas 2003.

I have indeed become a juggler. The biggest ball in the air right now is my family, but the other balls are up there. "Sundays at Sojourners" has much potential, I travel and speak on a regular basis, I continue to have media opportunities in England, and I anticipate that when my boys are older, the priestly ball will once again take more of my time and energy. I was fortunate to have choices. I could have gone back to "work" as an employed priest and opted for childcare, as some of my friends have done. The great thing is that although I have chosen to be an "at-home" mom, the priest has not disappeared. I have discovered a wonderful integration of priesthood and motherhood that is immensely satisfying. There is a richness about my life right now that makes me thankful that I can have so much, if not all at once, that priesthood and motherhood have to offer.

Acknowledgments

The Woman Behind the Collar is my first book, and I am indebted to a number of people who convinced me I could write it, enabled it to happen, and encouraged me along the way.

I am very grateful to the archbishop of Canterbury, Dr. Rowan Williams, who found the time in his busy schedule to write such a thoughtful and interesting piece for the American edition of my book. Thanks go to Roy M. Carlisle, senior editor, and the whole team at the Crossroad Publishing Company for believing that Americans would like to read my book. In addition I would like to thank John Eagleson of ediType for his work with Roy and me on making British-isms understandable to American readers.

I am very grateful to my efficient and friendly team at HarperCollinsUK, Val Hudson, Monica Chakraverty, and Gina Sussens. They have been wonderful guides and advisers. I am also grateful to James Catford, who originally took me on as an author before his departure from HarperCollinsUK.

I also want to extend warm thanks to my friend Rose Berger in Washington, D.C., who cast her skillful editorial eye over my first draft and made it look presentable. Many thanks also go to other friends who at various stages read parts of the book and offered valuable advice: Marlene Hicken, Mary Ann Richardson, Anne Stevens, David Isherwood, Susie Sanders, Ruth Dearnley, Christina Rees, and Kim Hitch to name a few. Big thanks go to Dawn French for her friendship and generous support of this book, especially in writing the foreword for the UK edition.

I am deeply grateful to all those friends who, because of a part they have played in my life, appear in the book. To those friends who are surprised to find themselves somewhere in the midst of the story, or who are sorry not to, I seek your understanding.

Most of all I am grateful to my family. My parents enthusiastically read material from day one of writing, while my son Luke happily went to day care for two days a week while mummy went back home to "write her stories."

Finally, my biggest thanks go to my husband, Jim Wallis, an accomplished author himself, who supported, encouraged, and loved me every day as the book slowly emerged. I consider myself fortunate beyond measure to be married to my hero, the man I respect and love most in the world. It is the strength and confidence that I have received from him that has ultimately enabled me to write this book.

About the Author

Joy Carroll Wallis was one of the first women to be ordained into the priesthood of the Church of England. She grew up in South London and was a primary school teacher before receiving a calling to ministry in the church. Joy was a spokesperson for the ordination of women, and served on the Church of England's General Synod as well as being the advisor to the popular comedy TV series *The Vicar of Dibley*. After ten years of inner-city ministry, she moved to live and work in an urban neighborhood of Washington, D.C., where she now lives with her husband, Jim Wallis, and their sons, Luke and Jackson.

The Reverend Joy Carroll Wallis today.

About the Publisher

The Crossroad Publishing Company seeks to contribute to the richness of life with fine books as a leader in spiritual, religious, and cultural publishing. We value the people with whom we work, our colleagues and our authors, all of whom we welcome as partners in our common venture.

It is an even stronger partnership when an editor is privileged to work with a priest of his own denomination on a book of keen insight and spiritual adventure. And it is even more exciting when that priest is married to one of the editor's best friends and most valued authors. Over the years I have had the pleasure of getting to know Joy as she and Jim Wallis have married — what a great honor it was to participate in the wedding party in London — and have begun to raise a family. Joy had previously followed her call to priesthood, first in the Anglican communion and now as an Episcopalian in the U.S. As a woman of uncommon intelligence and grace, Joy brings a deep Christian spiritual perspective to every dimension of her life. She is an inspiration both to her husband and her two young boys, and to all of us men and women who are privileged to call her friend.

In the midst of her busy life, Joy has been discovering her own voice as a writer. And in her writing we find not only her deeply spiritual and wise voice but also her rapier wit and vigorous sense of humor. Humor is the saving grace for many who take on the challenging task of pastoring those of us who remain laypeople in search of God's presence today. This humor, woven throughout this memoir, makes our journey with Joy even more enjoyable.

We are proud to add this delightful memoir by Joy Carroll Wallis to our esteemed list of Crossroad titles. As with other recent spiritual memoirs from Crossroad — including Steve Kissing's *Running from the Devil,* C. McNair Wilson's *Raised in Captivity,* Rita Winters's *The Green Desert,* Deal Hudson's *An American Conversion,* Paula D'Arcy's *Gift of the Red Bird,* John Killinger's *Ten Things I Learned Wrong from a Conservative Church,* Jean Gould's *Forty Years Since My Last Confession,* and Sarah Stockton's *Restless in Christ,* in this book you will find nurture for your soul in the author's warm and personal reflection on the vicissitudes of life and the subtle workings of the Spirit. We all need friends and guides along the Way and, as we know, books can be our guides and friends, as they have been for millions of Christians over many centuries.

ROY M. CARLISLE
Senior Editor

Lent 2004

Of Related Interest

James Alison
ON BEING LIKED

Homosexuality and religion is on the front pages again, with the June 2003 Supreme Court decision, the legalization of gay marriage in parts of Canada, and divisive debates in the Catholic and Anglican churches. James Alison, the world's most respected gay theologian and speaker, offers nine popular essays on the gay/Catholic controversies.

0-8245-2261-3, $18.95 paperback

Geralyn Wolf
DOWN AND OUT IN PROVIDENCE
Seeing Christianity through New Eyes

In this book, Bishop Wolf hails the beginning of a new phase of compassion rekindled. Using as the starting point her own thirty-day experience taking on the identity of a homeless person, and drawing from her involvement with the famed Taizé community in France, she invites us into a new reflection of how our spiritual lives can intersect with our social mission of compassion and caring. Designed for personal and group reflection, this book includes profound observations about our call as Christians as well as practical suggestions for living out the mission of a compassionate faith.

0-8245-2276-1, $16.95 paperback

crossroad

Of Related Interest

Rowan A. Greer
**CHRISTIAN HOPE
AND CHRISTIAN LIFE**
Raids on the Inarticulate

*Voted "Book of the Year" by the
Association of Theological Booksellers!*

What is the destiny of the human soul in this life and the next? Dare we hope to "see God face to face," or will our vision of God remain forever filtered "through a glass, darkly"?

In this remarkable volume, Rowan A. Greer turns to the New Testament, the church fathers, and later writers to throw light on their own visions of the human soul. He suggests that Augustine of Hippo and Gregory of Nyssa represent two distinct strands of Christian thinking that find expression later in writers such as John Donne and Jeremy Taylor.

Greer, who has trained two generations of historians and theologians in the rich thought of the early church, has succeeded in writing a volume that is both full of original scholarly insight and, by virtue of his elegant writing, accessible to laypeople and non-specialists.

0-8245-1916-7, $24.95 paperback

crossroad

Of Related Interest

Miriam Therese Winter
OUT OF THE DEPTHS
The Story of Ludmila Javorova, Roman Catholic Priest

The never-before-told true story of a courageous woman ordained in the Roman Catholic underground church during the religious persecutions of the communist era.

"This is a story that needs to be told. It is the story of a democratic, participatory, and prophetic church emerging in Czechoslovakian Catholicism at a moment of crisis and creativity, a church that chose to ordain women. Miriam Therese Winter is to be thanked for her gripping narration of this important story." — Rosemary Radford Ruether

"We need not theorize any longer about what women priests might do for the church. Miriam Therese Winter shows us Ludmila Javorova in action, ministering to the people of God in ways that few men could, as a clandestine priest in the underground Church of Czechoslovakia. This profoundly Catholic book has a bonus: a stunning portrait of a bishop with guts, Felix Davidek, Ludmila's mentor and the man who ordained her, despite opposition from the faint of heart. — Robert Blair Kaiser, contributing editor for *Newsweek*

0-8245-1889-6, $19.95 hardcover

Also available in Spanish
Desde lo hondo

0-8245-1975-2, $19.95 paperback

crossroad

Of Related Interest

James Alison
FAITH BEYOND RESENTMENT
Fragments Catholic and Gay

Responding to the Catholic Church's description of homosexuality as "objectively disordered," James Alison asks the question, "Why gays? Why now?" Through a close reading of scripture — especially the Gospel of John — he pieces together a daring image of "God as brother" that seeks to liberate gays from resentment toward Catholic teaching and restore the universal, inclusive message of Christ to church teaching.

"*Faith Beyond Resentment* is James Alison's boldest book yet, and in some ways his best yet."
— Rowan Williams, Archbishop of Canterbury,
in the *London Tablet*

0-8245-1922-1, $18.95 paperback

crossroad